I0415106

THE RED PILL

The Cure for Today's
Mass Media Culture

Harold Hay

ISBN-10: 1456566091
ISBN-13: 978-1456566098

Cover Design by John Calhoun

CONTENTS

ACKNOWLEDGMENTS

My warmest thanks and gratitude to my wife, Karen. Without her help, dedication, support, love and encouragement, this book would not be possible.

FOREWORD

We live in a time like no other in history. It can be the worst of times and the best of times. Never has mankind had so much vying for his attention. Knowledge and technology abound. Life for most of us is lived in the fast lane whether that's our intention or not.

Everywhere we turn, we are bombarded with images, enticements, and distractions. Living a quiet, unhindered Christian life is a thing of the past. Media, iPods, iPhones and social media seem to have taken over our lives.

Jesus said he has given us power to overcome the world, but we seem to be more overwhelmed today than ever. And what about reaching the world with the love of God? I believe God is telling us to refocus, rearm and change our way of thinking. God has a new game plan and a new arsenal he wants to put at our disposal. God wants to turn the tables on the devil who has had a hay day, using every device, technology and strategy to turn mankind away from God, and his strategy is working.

In the following pages you will learn about the media culture crisis and how you can be a part in turning our culture around. We are all called to the Great Commission. And with the call, God always provides the empowerment. We all have a part to play no matter how small that part is. Get ready to enter a whole new realm and see God use media and entertainment to speak into people's lives about his Truth and reveal his glory.

INTRODUCTION

The last thing I ever planned to do was write a book. In July 2009, I was let go from a Christian media ministry that I started in 1988. You hear stories about people losing their ministries, but you never think of it happening to you. Now what do you do? Start over? I have been working in the media for over 25 years. I have done just about everything including writing, editing, directing, and producing. God called me to start a media ministry and produce television programs that will point young people to Christ and that will encourage young Christians in their walk with God. I believed I could use television to reach people for Christ. I still do.

At the end of my time with the ministry that I founded, one of my shows was on over 200 stations and 15 networks worldwide. It was making an impact. God had also moved me to start teaching young people about media making and filmmaking. We started a film program for high school students. God had planted the seeds in my heart some years ago after reading Bob Reiner's book, <u>Roaring Lambs</u>, where he said that we needed to send young people into mainstream Hollywood and the entertainment industry to be media missionaries. I believed in the idea of reseeding our culture with a Biblical message by using movies, television programs and every other form of media. It was my dream to start a school dedicated to raising up, equipping and training future filmmakers as media missionaries.

But it all came to an end. In life, things change. Ministries, just like people, move on. They can evolve into something completely different than what you had in mind when you started out. I decided to start a new ministry and continue my work. My plan was to continue on, revamp my show and build a school dedicated to the development of media missionaries. But a lack of resources made this increasingly difficult. People I thought were going to help and be part of this plan failed to materialize. Was I following God's plan?

I decided that the easiest path was to create an online school and a website to discuss the role and purpose of media missionaries, so I launched <u>mediamissionaryschool.com</u>. But, again, resources didn't come in to develop the website. Nor did we have the funds to properly promote the site. The plan just wasn't working. But God is always at work even when we don't quite understand his plan.

Writing has never been a passion of mine. I only do it because it is necessary. Some of my colleagues convinced me that it was time to start writing a blog. This would give me an opportunity to speak on media issues as it relates to faith. I've spent the better part of 20 years trying to understand the media culture and how it is impacting our faith. So I started writing and writing and writing. And after a few weeks, it became clear that God was at work. He gave me a passion to write. The words just kept coming, and I realized they were not mine but God's. Each day I went out on my usual run, and God revealed himself and gave me ideas. As I continued to run each day, ideas just kept coming. As I said, I never started out to write a book, but it's become clear that this is what God wanted me to do. God was at work, and he was inviting me to join him.

He always has a plan. And, most often, it's not our plan or the way we would do things. I'm convinced that God wants a school for media missionaries, but his first objective is to get this book out. I have been asking God for years what a media culture is. How is it influencing us? How are these things connected? When is somebody going to write a book to put all of the pieces together? It became clear that God wanted me to do it. What you are about to read is not from me. I believe it's from God. He has given me a plan and has helped me to put the pieces together.

If you are concerned about the direction of our culture and how it is impacting you, your children and your grandchildren, you need to read this book. This is a book of hope and a book of promise. Yes, the in culture is a crisis, but it is also an opportunity. But only if we seize the moment. We have the power through God to change our world. I will share with you five core principles that I am convinced will change everything.

Anything is possible as long as we have not lost faith. When we stop believing that change is possible and believe that the problems are too complex, there really is no hope. There are solutions to the media culture crisis, if we explore the opportunities that God is giving us. He, as I have stated, is already at work. He is working in the media culture, and he is working in the lives of those who live and function in the church of media and entertainment. I believe you will find this book thought-provoking and that it will challenge the conventional wisdom of how we see Hollywood and the entertainment industry.

Is there a plan and a strategy to reach people living in this age? How is God at work in the entertainment industry? What kind of stories does God want us to tell? What is a media missionary? I'm convinced that what God has given me in this book will shed light on these questions and provide answers. All of us will have a role in solving the media culture crisis.

I believe that God gave me this book for everybody in the Body of Christ. I'm sure most of us are not planning to go to Hollywood to make films or television programs. But the media culture must be our concern and our issue. It's vital to our future. Every one is impacted by the increasing power of today's media culture.

This book is especially for you if God has put a burden on your heart to use media for his glory. Perhaps, you have been making short films for years, or you may be a student in film school. How do you combine your passion for Christ and your passion for media making? Have you been called by God to be a media missionary? This is a book you must read. I'm convinced it will give you insight into your calling as well as how you can be used by God in the film and media industry.

If you're ready to start a new journey, discover how God is working in the media, and to grab hold of those new opportunities to reach a generation that is defined by today's media culture, read on.

1   The Red Pill

Most of us have seen the 1999 film, The Matrix, starring Keanu Reeves as Neo. In the movie's most critical scene, Neo faces a difficult choice between taking the red pill or the blue pill. I think we all face the same decision in our daily lives. We just don't realize it. In Neo's world, life is good, safe, predictable and convenient. Sound familiar? But the world he lives in that he believes is real is actually a fabrication and doesn't exist.

The blue pill allows him the opportunity to go on and live his life in this artificial or contrived reality. The red pill will offer him the chance to see things as they actually are. Once he takes the red pill, there is no going back. He will have to face the truth no matter how unpleasant or unpredictable. It will require him to think for himself and be accountable for his actions. So Neo rejects the status quo and takes the red pill.

The Matrix started me thinking. What would we do if we were faced with the same decision? Is the world we live in and the life we live real? Or has it been created by an outside force? Most of us will never be faced with a choice that is this black and white. But it is an intriguing question. Would we take the red pill if it offered us real answers? If we could understand the reasoning behind the decisions we make and if we could understand the basis of what we believe and why we believe it, would we take the red pill?

If you've read my blog, you probably realize that I believe that the world we accept as normal is manipulated and controlled by today's mass media culture. In other words, the world you and I live in is a reflection of today's media and the reality it has created. I'm convinced most of us probably wouldn't take the red pill because, frankly, the truth is just too scary. And I believe the majority of us think we already know and understand the world we live in so there's no need to take the red pill. However, I'm not sure that's the case.

The media has done a snow job on our culture. The media has been successful in helping to distract and insulate us from the realities of life and the things that are truly important. Our mass media culture reflects this. It has created its own matrix, and, for the most part, we have bought into it. I would go as far to say that the media culture has rewired our brains and the way we think.

The lives you and I live today take place in the marketplace. Everything is now a form of buying and selling. Life itself has been commercialized. How we make money seems to always be our first priority. Our existence seems to be driven by a never-ending appetite for consumerism. More is better. We must have everything and have it now seems to be the message that today's media is communicating. Even the American Dream has been hijacked and perverted by this form of consumerism. Our lives are also defined by advertising, marketing and branding. We become the products that we use or consume. We are told that the next purchase will make us the person we have always wanted to become.

The ultimate goal of life itself is to achieve celebrity, to become important and successful no matter what the cost. Does any of this sound familiar? Are we on a treadmill with no hope of ever getting off? Perhaps the red pill can offer us hope to escape this false reality. Today's mass media culture has placed you and I at the center of our own world. Everything revolves around our wants and needs. It has helped to reinforce our own self-importance along with instant gratification of wealth, power and prestige. Would you agree that this is in direct contrast to the basic, simple teachings of Christ? As difficult as this may be to accept, we have all to some degree bought into the mass media culture. That includes people of faith.

Breaking out of this stranglehold will be no easy endeavor. Who doesn't want a lifestyle or even a Christian faith that is safe, convenient, comfortable and puts us in control? However, that is not what the Word of God has called us to nor is it the reality of the Christian faith. Symbolically, we can continue to take the blue pill, but this leads us away from what God intends for us.

So if you decide to take the red pill and start down this road where you begin to think for yourself and to question everything, there is no turning back. Nothing will ever be the same again. The Bible says the truth will set you free. But do you want to know the truth, and do you really want to be free? I guarantee you, there will be a price to pay for this freedom.

2 Today's Media Culture and The Perfect Storm

I write a substantial number of articles revolving around the subject of the media culture. But what exactly is a media culture? Media is pretty straightforward. Practically any form of electronic entertainment makes up the media. This would include television programs, movies, internet content, video games, news and virtually all other forms of electronic images.

The concept of culture is complex. It certainly involves more than going to the opera. Culture is a shared consciousness of a particular society. It influences our behaviors, attitudes, actions, thought patterns and beliefs. Its influence is direct and indirect as well as tangible and intangible. Culture, by its nature, helps to define our worldview and point-of-view. This process helps to interpret the world around us and acts as a lens through which we view politics, religion, philosophy, and lifestyle choices. Culture also plays a major part in the development of our institutions, such as government, schools, and churches.

Culture provides the framework where society functions and operates. Obviously, not everyone within our culture thinks alike or has the same view of our world. But culture provides a baseline or foundation where acceptable behaviors or customs are allowed to occur.

In theory, culture should drive and define our society. That's the way it has worked throughout the history of mankind. But in the past few decades, something unique has happened to America. Culture should drive media, but today we live in a society where media defines and creates culture. That's why I call it a media culture. In fact, the two are indistinguishable from each other. It's impossible to determine where media ends or culture begins.

Wikipedia's encyclopedia says that a perfect storm is an expression that describes an event where a rare combination of circumstances will aggravate a situation drastically [1]

When a series of events came together at the right time and place in our nation's history, they created a perfect storm, which caused media to be transformed into a force capable of creating a media culture. What rare combination of circumstances has made the media a significant and powerful force in our culture? When did television, movies and other forms of media stop being entertainment and become a media culture capable of shaping our beliefs, attitudes and behaviors?

The media culture has had the added effect where we have created a society that is more uniform and harmonious. I'm convinced we are far more compliant and willing to conform to the central message driving today's media culture. Many may argue how this is possible in light of a society which seems to be divided. Obviously, there is a great debate about the future of America. There seems to be a great divide between Democrats, Republicans, Liberals, Conservatives and Progressives. There is also a generational divide between baby boomers and millennials. But are we really that different in our philosophy and thinking?

I believe that below the surface of our public discord we will find a society that is far more influenced and controlled by the media culture than anyone can possibly believe. Although we may express our feelings and viewpoints differently, we are motivated by the same forces. Whether we are on the right or the left, we have embraced a philosophy that positions us in the center of our own universe. Without a doubt, this is the core message of today's media culture.

So some questions remain. Why do we have a media culture? Who benefits from it? And what proof can I offer to you of its existence and impact? First, why we have a media culture is a very long story. In Appendix 1, I explain the origins and the development of our current modern media culture.

The short answer is the rapid development of technology has made the media culture a reality. Without television, satellite communications, cable TV, computers, internet, cell phones, iPads, iPhones and mobile media devices, the media culture would not exist. As a result, technology has led us from a word-based to an image-based society. Images dominate practically every aspect of our lives. Images also communicate powerful messages that we are often not aware of because they impact us on the subconscious level. You may be familiar with the old saying "a picture is worth a thousand words." In today's society, it's probably worth 10,000 words or more. Just like a moth that is attracted to the light, we are attracted to images. Our brains are wired in such a way that we think visually and are stimulated by visual images. This helps to explain why reading is decreasing in our society. Because of the power of images, it's easy to understand why we spend 8 hours a day involved with media.

Those who finance and create images have seen an opportunity. By controlling the images we view, they have created a consumer-based society. We now live in a society where perception is more important than reality. In order to increase the effectiveness of the impact of consumerism on the individual, marketers, advertisers and branders have found a way to associate images with their goods and services in order to sell us an image of what they say we should desire to be and to own. Of course, none of this is based in reality.

Second, business primarily benefits from the existence of a media culture. In order to maximize profits, business must control the culture. But business cannot do this without the help and support of the media. It's through the use and the manipulation of the media that business controls and dominates our culture.

Don't get me wrong. I am not one to believe in conspiracies. No, I don't believe that aliens crashed in Roswell in 1947 and the United States government participated in a massive cover-up. Nor do I believe in Bigfoot. And I certainly do not believe that JFK was assasinated by the CIA or the FBI. And I don't believe business leaders gather to discuss how they are going to dominate and control our culture in order to sell us their goods and products. Whether intentionally, unintentionally or organically, a media culture has emerged in our society.

What evidence can I offer you? I believe I could get a conviction in any court of law through direct and circumstantial evidence wherein I'm convinced no one could possibly have reasonable doubt as to the existence of a media culture and its impact on our society. Here are my ten arguments.

1. We are defined by what we own and not by our character. You may not be a fan of President Jimmy Carter or his politics, but President Carter made a profound statement in the late 1970s where he said we are defined by what we own and not by what we do. The truth is that in our society today character doesn't matter. We are defined by the house we live in, the car we drive, the clothes we wear, the schools and colleges we send our kids to and the church we attend.

    The question is who are we as a people? Have we lost our identity to the things we own? How we acted and how we treated people used to define us. It seems that character has become an obstacle to our success and the ability to achieve. Is it possible that our media culture has helped us to embrace this view.

2. All media has become some form of marketing. Today every aspect of our life is lived in the "marketplace". No space exists between our lives and marketing, advertising, and branding. It surrounds and engulfs us. Everything within our society has been commercialized. How do we make money? That's the first question that's

often asked in practically everything we do. The "marketplace" concept helps to explain why every sports arena or stadium now has a corporate sponsor tied to the name of the facility.

3. Consumerism is king. Has there ever been a society that has embraced consumerism as we have here in America? In fact, we invented it. Our big-box stores are full of merchandise beckoning to be bought. But do we really need all of the stuff? We are encouraged to spend, spend, spend. After the tragedy of 9/11, even President George W. Bush encouraged the American people to do their patriotic duty by going shopping.

Our economy would collapse without maximum spending by the American public. We have built a society based on consumerism. We have boxed ourselves in. We are not encouraged to save but to spend. Only a media culture could convince us to accept this idea.

4. Runaway debt. Not only are we encouraged to spend, but we are equally encouraged to charge, charge, charge. They make it easy. Swipe that card. Individual credit card debt is out of control in our society. We hear so much criticism of our politicians who have run up record-breaking deficits. But, in reality, we all have engaged in the same practice. Congress is no different than the general American public. We want everything. And if we can't afford it, we just put it on credit. The media culture has helped form a narrative that has made this practice acceptable and convenient.

5. The redefining of the American Dream. For decades we all have debated about the origin and the definition of the American Dream. For many the American Dream is about family, home ownership, justice, freedom/security and fair play. But many argue that today the American Dream is more about wealth, power, materialism and consumerism. Today we believe in a "bigger is better" concept. I'm convinced that today's media culture manipulates images from the traditional American Dream to create a new mythology that supports and reinforces a new American Dream which says that we deserve to have it all. Therefore, the American Dream must always be expanded. It's not enough to own two cars. Now each member of the family must have a car. There's no stopping this expansionist view even if it's detrimental to the development of our society. Those who argue against this concept or believe that we should live within our means or live with less receive severe criticism.

6. A new value system is being created. What values are being communicated in our media culture? What's important to us, and what occupies our time and interests? Today our media stars have been embraced and turned into gods. We are in love with celebrity. But what really motivates us? What we seek is what celebrity represents, which is power, wealth and fame. This is the new value system that preoccupies our society. Movie stars, athletes, models, and TV personalities are who we emulate and desire to be.

   But what about those who contribute the most to society such as teachers, public servants, and social workers? Are they as well paid or are they exalted to the same level of celebrity? How we view celebrity reveals a great deal about who we are as a people.

7. We no longer have a moral compass. There was a time when there was a clear right and wrong. Today's modern media culture has convinced us that everything is ambiguous. Therefore, the individual must decide what is right or wrong based on current circumstances. How else can you explain millions of abortions since the early 1970s or the fact that over 40% of children born in the United States are from unwed mothers? Only a media culture could explain the rapid collapse of basic moral principles that have occurred in a relatively short time.

8. Judeo-Christian ideas and philosophy are fading. Whether or not America was ever a Christian nation, our nation was most certainly based and established on Judeo-Christian concepts. Whether you are a Christian or not, historically you respected the integrity and truth of the Judeo-Christian message. That's no longer true today. We are moving from a Judeo-Christian society and transforming into something completely different. No one can say with any certainty what that will look like.

9. The rapid rate of change. Culture, in and of itself, changes over the course of time like a meandering river. In other words, it takes time for change to occur. Within a media culture, change is rapid and sudden. Isn't that the world we currently live in? Worldviews seem to change like the shifting sands. Nothing is solid. Obviously, technology plays a part in this rapid and ever-changing

media culture in which we find ourselves. But it is the ideas that really drive the forces of change.

10. The psychology of selling. We are convinced that our next buying purchase will truly lead us to fulfillment and happiness. Today's marketing is enormously complex and dependent on psychological manipulation. A product today has the ability to transform and define our lives. We become the person we have always wanted to be through the use of the product. It can make us look younger or older. Or it can create the image that we wish to project. In some ways, we become the product. In fact, our lifestyle is based on its use. Only a media culture could create this type of influence and impact.

When we think of the media or try to understand it, we don't view it in terms of a media culture but as the images on our widescreen televisions or the images projected in our multiplexes. The media and the general concept of a media culture is much more than this. The media culture can be a difficult concept to embrace, but its existence is as real as the air we breathe. Think of it as an invisible force that surrounds us. In some ways, it affects every part of our lives and the choices we make. Just like radiation, we cannot see it, feel it, touch it or taste it. But the media culture is just as real as the damaging effects from low dosages of radiation. Both have the ability to change us from the inside out.

I have presented the evidence. Now that we understand that the media culture has a tremendous impact on society, the question is what can we do to change our current situation.

3 The Real News—The Rise of the Media Church

Do you want to know what the most important story was in the Cincinnati Enquirer on January 20, 2010? Hopefully, you still read the newspaper. It wasn't found on the front page. No, it's not the story of the Republican, Scott Brown, Senatorial victory in Massachusetts over the once-favored Democrat, Martha Coakley. The most important story was found somewhere near the back section of the newspaper. It's an inconspicuous three columns titled, *Kids Spend Nearly Eight Hours a Day on Electronic Media.*[2]

You might be asking yourself, "Is that really news"? Absolutely. The problem is that nobody is paying attention. The story is based on a new study by the Kaiser Family Foundation. They have been tracking this type of data for years. What they have found is that today's kids are now spending 53 hours a week in front of some type of electronic media. That includes cell phones, iPods, video games, and computers, which averages out to 7 hours, 38 minutes per day.

Just ten years ago, the average time was 6 hours, 19 minutes. That's 79 more minutes of free time each day listening to music, watching TV and movies, and playing video games. The study also found that 20% of kids' media now comes from mobile media devices. And that's likely to increase in the years ahead. Vicky Rideout, who is the director of the study program, states, "Electronic media is part of the air that kids breathe." I'd say that's the understatement of the decade. The findings are based on research from over 2,000 participants ages 8-18. There's plenty of other findings, but the real question is, "What does it all mean?" Or perhaps maybe we should ask, "Does anybody really care?"[3] We all know that our kids are spending a tremendous amount of their time consuming some form of media every day.

I've spent 25 years researching the topic of how media influences our culture and youth. What I have found is that most people are somewhat indifferent. Deep down they understand there's a problem. Sure, they find some things in the media troubling, but they are just not sure what to do. So, in many cases, they do nothing.

More importantly, how are Christian leaders and parents responding? The response so far has been disappointing. Why? Because for the most part the Church has its head stuck in the sand. We don't want to admit that the media has this type of power, control and influence. We all are consumed with electronic media. And if we address the issue with our kids, then we must admit that we are in the same boat. And that makes us uncomfortable.

The reality of our situation is that media has become a new church, more powerful than anything we could imagine.

It goes well beyond bad language, sex, violence and nudity. Media now extends itself out from the electronic screen. It has infiltrated our lives and culture. It is part of everything we absorb on some level. It has influenced how we think, where we go, what we do and what's important.

Let's say that the average, committed Christian teenager goes to church twice weekly, including being an active participant in the youth ministry. That's maybe four hours a week, tops. Let's say for the sake of argument that he or she may even go on a mission trip or two. Now compare that to the amount and level of media that they are exposed to each week. Think about it. Really think about it. Who do you think is going to win?

Some studies have found that over 70% of teens in youth ministry will abandon their faith after age 18. Again, who's winning the battle? Most Christian leaders don't want to talk about this. That's the real story.

I'm a media guy. And I know that media, including films and TV, can have a profound, positive impact. That's why I am encouraging Christians to get serious about this issue. We need to teach our kids to be media savvy, to make good choices, and to understand the messages and the influence of today's media culture. That can be done through a solid media literacy program. We need to teach youth to think for themselves and not allow the media to think for them. I know this seems overwhelming, but this is a place to start.

Getting back to the article, Vicky Rideout's final thoughts are very appropriate. "Anything that takes up this much time, we really do need to think about it and talk about it."[4] Are you ready to start a dialogue?

The Media Church

The media culture has created a new church and a new place of worship that is without a physical address. Its members are unaware that this new church exists or that they are a part of it. It is America's fastest growing church—the church of media and entertainment.

The members of this church are searching for the truth, but they must experience truth in order for it to be authentic. They are highly influenced by postmodern philosophy. They seek connectivity and two-way communication. They desire to express their views and opinions about life and interact with those who have different views. Social media and YouTube are an intricate part of their lives because they want to be involved in the process. That's why many in this church make and distribute their own media. They are searching for the truth but do not want to be told what the truth is. They seek a safe place where it's easy for them to fit in and where they are not required to do anything.

Whether you realize it or not, the media culture crisis does exist. However, the majority of the population believes it is nothing more than trivial entertainment or harmless popular culture. But I believe this media culture is in crisis. And for committed Christians who are concerned about their faith, it is undoubtedly a crisis for us because Christianity is losing its impact on the culture. Media and culture have merged to create a *media culture*. By doing so, it is capable of controlling the hearts and minds of this generation. More importantly, the media culture is moving into a position where it will potentially control the direction of Christianity. But perhaps the greatest crisis we face is when we fail to respond to the opportunity the media culture crisis presents to the Church.

What opportunity does the media culture present? First it's important to note that today's media consumption per week is somewhere between 50 to 60 hours. Teenagers will typically spend up to 8 hours a day consuming some form of electronic media. It's clear to see what has their attention. The majority of the population is interested in movies, television, mobile media and every other form of electronic communication. This segment of the population lives and breathes within the church of media and entertainment.

Since we now have a media culture that is capable of shaping attitudes, beliefs and behaviors that lead people away from God, then it is just as capable of being used in a manner that will lead them toward God. We need to realize that God is already at work in the media culture and the church of media and entertainment. All he requires is for us to join him in his work.

How do we build a bridge to engage them? Is it possible that they are finding a more profound spiritual and satisfying experience in the media? If we are going to engage this church, we must understand what makes it a church. First, it's impossible to deny the power, size and scope of today's media institutions. They are the pillars of today's media and entertainment church. Five multimedia conglomerates dominate and control the cross-promotion and selling of today's media culture to our society. CBS Corporation, formerly Viacom, Time Warner, NBC Universal, Walt Disney and News Corp produce over 80% of media and entertainment produced in North America. Each company has its own film, broadcasting, news cable outlet, publishing, internet, and music interests. Combine that with over 700 motion pictures being produced in Hollywood yearly and 300 broadcast and cable networks, and you can understand the magnitude and power of today's media. In fact, the real center of power no longer resides in Washington D.C. It can be found in the boardrooms of these five multimedia conglomerates. They can dictate what is important as well as what is not important. Their decisions not only influence culture but also make culture.

Second, our society and culture have created a symbiotic relationship with media and entertainment. They are dependant on each other. In some ways, we find our value and purpose in the media we consume. It helps to define who we are as a person. Our identity is therefore a part of the relationship that we have with our entertainment and media choices. We are what we consume. The real nature of this relationship can be found in the roots of consumerism. Media and entertainment are tied to the marketplace of ideas. However, in reality, there is only one idea that fuels this relationship. That is the buying and selling of media and entertainment produced by the five major multimedia conglomerates. This idea becomes a religion because it promotes a lifestyle and a belief system that enables us to see the need and the desire to embrace whatever entertainment and media they market and promote.

Finally, the church of media and entertainment is a legitimate church because it shares many of the characteristics of our own Christian tradition. That includes having a god, an experience, structure, a belief system, an ultimate truth, worship, community/fellowship, customs and rituals, a sense of purpose, a vision, a bible, a place of origin in history and a hierarchy.

A God

The church of media and entertainment has many gods which could include technology, movies, a director, an actor or could more likely be yourself. You determine who your god will be. But whatever choice you make, he will be on your side and interested in meeting your needs. Your god is accessible and available at all times.

An Experience

Members in this church seek a profound experience. It can be found in technology, consuming media or making media. They seek a relationship with the experience; therefore, they want it to be interactive so that they are a part of it. The experience should be capable of meeting and fulfilling whatever the emotional need.

Structure, Belief System and Ultimate Truth

Members in this church are looking for answers. In one way or another they are asking questions about the nature and purpose of life. Media provides the structure in which they can ask questions. Although there are many belief systems expressed in media and entertainment, it is possible to find one that fits into your philosophical approach to life. Beliefs can be expressed in movies and on television or any other new form of new media. By consuming media, they are looking for an experience which will lead to some form of truth.

Worship

Worship can take place any time, anywhere. Worship is an act of praise or honor to a god or gods. Worship can also be defined as being in the presence of your god or gods. Members of the church of media engage in the act of worship when they interact with any form of media. This can happen at a movie theater, at home or in front of the internet. Worship is continuous and ongoing.

Community/Fellowship

Members of the church of media and entertainment have a profound need to be connected—to be a part of something which leads to social interaction. Fellowship can occur not only while watching media but while talking about media. What was your experience? What do you think the movie was saying? What did you think about the character? Social media provides the perfect framework for the need to engage in community and fellowship.

Customs and Rituals

Going to a movie theater can be a ritual in itself. The experience can provide a rich texture of sights and sounds. Buttery popcorn and the comforting feel of a reclining chair are part of the rituals and just as important as the movie. Rituals are also performed in other forms of consumption, including watching your favorite television show or engaging in activity that makes you comfortable, such as certain drinks, food, or other preparations. Customs can also be found in the

Academy Awards and other iconic images of the entertainment industry.

A Sense of Purpose

We wrongly assume that media is just entertainment. Members of this church can find purpose in the media through the process of interacting with media, technology, friends, and the experiences it creates. The media in and of itself becomes a purpose.

A Vision

Members of this church are searching for a lifestyle and a worldview that make their lives meaningful. Because media is so diverse, it is possible to find a vision that makes you comfortable. Your vision may not necessarily be about changing the world but may be about creating a life that makes you feel good about yourself. It offers a sense of completeness.

A Bible

The church of media has a bible. It is their stories—the stories shared in movies, television and every other form of electronic media. Most find a form of truth that helps to define their beliefs, attitudes, and worldview.

A Place of Origin in History

The Mecca for the church of media and entertainment is Hollywood. All things holy exist and dwell in this strange faraway land. The entire history of the entertainment industry, for the most part, has taken place in a small geographical area in and around the hills of Hollywood.

A Hierarchy

The church of media has its own leaders and people of influence. It starts with producers, directors, actors, writers, cinematographers, and so on. These people have an enormous influence on the members of the church of media. They are looked upon with great respect, and their opinions can be taken as the authority and power of a god.

It's hard not to see that the church of media and entertainment functions in a similar fashion as the Church. So how do we maximize our opportunities that the media culture crisis presents? First, we must acknowledge that the media church is legitimate and does not have to pose a threat to Christianity. Not everything expressed in the media church is necessarily bad or evil. Second, we need to start a dialogue. By talking to them, we can better understand what they are seeking. Honest, two-way communication can turn a crisis into the best opportunity that Christians have in our current age. Third, we need to find common ground. I'm sure if we understood the media culture and this new church, we would be able to discover our commonalities that can provide the basis for establishing a relationship. Finally, this relationship will enable us to foster trust that will give us access to the broader media culture. If we remain apart from the church of media and entertainment, how will we reach them? How will they discover and understand God's truth or his plan for their lives? We have an opportunity to interact with a new generation that has embraced a lifestyle based in media, entertainment and technology.

Paul gave us a model that follows this strategy in Acts 17:22-23. Paul traveled to Athens and recognized the legitimacy of the counsel of philosophers. He started a dialogue by saying, "Men of Athens, I see that in every way you are very religious. For as I walked around and looked carefully at your objects of worship, I even found an altar with this inscription: TO AN UNKNOWN GOD. Now what you worship as something unknown, I am going to proclaim to you." *(NIV)* Paul started a discussion which resulted in interaction with the counsel. He did not condemn but sought common ground. The scripture goes on to say, "For in him we live and move and exist, as one of your own poets says 'we are his off spring'. And since this is true, we shouldn't think of God as an idol designed by craftsmen from gold or silver or stone." *(NIV)* Paul was brilliant because he found common ground by acknowledging this legitimate truth. He was then able to use that to point out where the counsel of philosophers was mistaken and was then able to share with them about the one true God.

Christians today can use the same strategy that Paul has given us to engage the media culture and the media church. Romans 1:14 says, "For I have a great sense of obligation for people in our culture and to people in other cultures to the educated and uneducated alike. So I am eager to come to you in Rome, too, to preach God's Good News." *(NLT)* Paul went to the centers of power during his time, which included Rome and Athens. He felt an obligation to bring the Gospel to other cultures, other points of view, people with different philosophies and with a different understanding of what they consider the truth to be.

Today's center of power is in Hollywood and the entertainment industry. We have the same opportunity in our age to engage a different culture and a different people. Our goal is to reach the church of media and entertainment. By doing so, we can affect and change the course of today's media culture. By proclaiming the Truth, we set the stage for reestablishing the moral authority of God in our society. Christianity doesn't have to lose its influence in the culture. We can have a positive impact on the attitudes, behaviors and beliefs for generations to come. By establishing a relationship with our culture, we will lead many to find Christ. Our opportunities are many. God is already at work. All he requires is for us to join him.

4   God is Still at Work

Those who are a part of the new church of media and entertainment worship an unknown god, but their unknown god is our God, the God who created the earth and sent his son, Jesus, to die for us that we would be reconciled to God. God is still at work in the world and in the church of media and entertainment. But how?

The Spirit of God

Acts 17:28 says, "By his power we live and move and exist." *(NCV)* That means the Spirit of God is active in and through the human spirit. We have to conclude that the sacred is present across all human endeavors. If that's the case, then why would his presence not be felt in the movies?

Genesis 1:26 says, "Then God said, 'Let us make human beings in our image and likeness. And let them rule over the fish in the sea and the birds in the sky, over the tame animals, over all the earth, and over all the small crawling animals on the earth.' So God created human beings in his own image. In the image of God he created them. he created them male and female." *(NCV)*

This scripture suggests that we are all capable of reflecting God's truth at some level. That helps to explain why people can encounter God in the so-called secular media. The Biblical account of Jonah offers some interesting insight into the Spirit of God working in man. Jonah is directed by God to go to the great city of Nineveh to proclaim his judgment. But Jonah refuses to obey God because he realizes the Lord is merciful, and he fears that God will not destroy the people of Nineveh. What's interesting about this story is how the Spirit of God works in those who do not serve God. Jonah boards a ship going to Tarshish. A great storm arises which causes the sailors to ask Jonah if he is responsible for the storm. Jonah informs them that he is running away from God. He tells the sailors that in order to stop the storm they must throw him into the sea. This offered the non-Hebrew and non-followers of God an easy out. But the sailors acted in a righteous manner by trying harder to row the boat ashore. They did not want to kill Jonah.

God's Spirit was obviously at work in the sailors' lives who cried out to Jonah's God and pleaded for him to not make them die for Jonah's sin. Finally they were forced to throw Jonah overboard. As the sea calms, the sailors were awestruck by God's great power, and they offered him a sacrifice and vowed to serve him. Jonah's disobedience against God was used to bring the sailors to repentance. The Spirit of God worked in all circumstances to fulfill his will. The fascinating aspect of Jonah's story is that unrighteous men acted more righteously than a righteous man, which caused a righteous man to finally accept God's will. Do you think that God can use filmmakers both Christian and non-Christian to fulfill his purpose?

God is Present

Some people might believe that God is no longer at work in the world. The fact is God never left. He is still in the process of creation. Each day is a new day and a new creation. God's presence can be felt throughout the world through his creation.

Genesis 1:31 says, "And God looked at everything he had made, and he saw that it was very good." *(NCV)* Romans 8:19 says, "Everything God made is waiting with excitement for God to show his children's glory completely." *(NCV)*

God is currently in the process of restoring creation back to excellence. He is not finished with this world or mankind. Therefore, his presence is actively at work in all things. Everything in the world reveals God's truth. That includes filmmaking and media making. Because it is a creative process, it mirrors God's love for creation and redemption. When we are creating, we are near God's heart because we are made in his image.

God Uses All Things

God can use all things for the fulfillment of his divine purposes. For example, movies or any form of media from non-Christian media makers or filmmakers, including elements we may find offensive, can contain God's divine truth and is capable of moving our hearts toward God. Romans 8:28 says, "And we know in all things God works for good to those who love God, who have been called according to his purpose." *(NIV)*

If we accept this concept that God uses all things to fulfill his purpose, that would suggest that God's grace is present throughout all of human culture. It illustrates the point that God can use filmmakers to speak both truth and untruth to fulfill his purpose. We cannot limit God's power or choose which way he will work. Our theology is not the ultimate source of truth. God is truth and will use anything he chooses and in whatever order he wishes to communicate his truth to mankind, including films that may offend us because they contain both truth and untruth. Jesus had this in mind in his parable of the wheat and the weeds.

In Matthew 13:24-30 Jesus says, "The Kingdom of heaven is like a man who sowed good seed in his field. But while everybody was sleeping, his enemy came and sowed weeds among the wheat and went away. When the wheat sprouted and formed heads, then the weeds also appeared. The owner's servant came and said to him, 'sir, didn't you sow good seed in your field? Where then did the weeds come from?' 'An enemy did this', he replied. The servant asked him, 'do you want us to go and pull them up?' 'No', he answered, 'because while you are pulling the weeds, you may root up the wheat with them. Let both grow together until the harvest. At that time I will tell the harvesters to first collect the weeds and tie them in bundles to be burned. Then gather the wheat and bring it into my barn'." *(NIV)*

God can use films which contain both the wheat and the weeds for our benefit. We should not reject the wheat (truth) because the weeds (untruth) are present. The servant wanted to pull the weeds out. But the master wanted the process to go forward because it would harm the wheat. When we watch movies, we are confronted with a decision. It is our harvesting time in which we must discern what is true and what is not. That's how God can use movies and media to speak to us. This gives us the opportunity to grow in our spiritual development as believers. It becomes obvious that the weeds are there for a purpose. In order to fully understand truth, we also have to understand and recognize the untruth.

When Jesus spoke this parable, He was culturally relevant to his audience, which was primarily an agricultural community. They could understand that wheat and weeds were metaphors for good and evil. But I also believe that Jesus was speaking to everyone, including us. He layered the parable with subtext and multiple layers of meaning that we could understand today in a primarily technical society.

We live in a world where both good and evil exist, along with truth and untruth. Jesus wants us to develop the ability to distinguish the difference between the two. The untruth or the things that are against God's will can be used to lead us to the truth. That's why I believe the farmer did not pull the weeds from the field. They served God's purpose.

Likewise, movies contain the truth and the untruth along with good and evil. We can develop skills to recognize the difference between the two just as we can distinguish the difference between wheat and weeds. We should not reject the weeds because they serve the purpose of bringing us to the ultimate truth of God's love.

So if God is using filmmakers to tell his stories, why are we not seeing more results that lead people to Christ? First, we have to stop judging Hollywood and blaming them for every social issue in America over the last 60 years. Second, we have to understand that the media culture crisis, in some way, is our own doing because we have failed to understand how God is at work in entertainment and media. We have withdrawn from what we consider to be secular art. We have discouraged our young people in pursuing careers in media and entertainment. However, we have embraced the main theme of media by accepting materialism and consumerism as a primary source in our lives. And finally, the secular filmmakers that have something important to say are few in number. When they create art that reflects God's glory, we should embrace it and encourage it. Unfortunately, that's not the case with the mainstream movie, *Magnolia*. This movie is a prime example where many Christians could not get past the language in the movie to see a greater truth that allowed us an opportunity to dialogue with those who are asking questions about forgiveness.

Can You Experience God at the Movies?

I know I have experienced God at the movies. He can use films to speak to us. Film is unique in all forms of media. There is something about the process that can transform truth into reality. *Wendy and Lucy* is a film that recently spoke to me. It is a story about a 20-something girl on a cross-country trip to Alaska. She is seeking a better life with her dog, Lucy. She has little resources or money. She hopes to find employment in the fishing industry. We don't know much about her life other than that she seems to have few choices. The trip represents an all-or-nothing attempt for Wendy to have some sort of life. Unfortunately, her car breaks down. She becomes stranded and has to leave her dog, whom she dearly loves. Her only option is to hop a freight train bound for an unknown destination. We really don't know in the film what becomes of Wendy. Will she be reunited with her dog? Will life's circumstances become more grueling? Could she end up dead?

It seems like a simple story, so why did it speak to me? What God was saying to me is that Wendy is one of his children. And we live in a world where nobody cares about them. They are invisible. We only care about the things that we are interested in and are unwilling to look at how life can be very ugly. In this movie, nobody really cared enough to reach out to her or to offer help. God was asking me, "What are you going to do about it?"

If God is speaking to me in the movies, I am sure he is speaking to others as well. Spend any time online, and you will find people talking about movies. Are they being impacted? Again, *Magnolia*, a movie from several years ago, had a profound impact on it's viewers. *Magnolia* has nine separate but interlocking stories. It takes place in one day in the San Fernando Valley in Los Angeles. It's a journey into the human condition. The central theme of the movie is that there is no past wrongdoing that cannot be undone and forgiven.

What did people say about it?

- The movie heals.

- The writer of the script had God on his mind and offered the healing of the human soul through forgiveness.

- It touched me in ways that I have never been touched before.

- It showed me sides of people that we need to see. What are we doing? Silently judging you? It was the director's slap of the audiences face through Tom Cruise's character that made me rethink how I view others. What do I really know about that person?

- This is a very thought-provoking film. It takes a while to process. It shows how faith in Christ can heal the effects of sin.

- It makes us question ourselves. Are we all that sick? Is society really that messed up?

- The last scene of the film touched me greatly, and I found myself almost in tears. The message of forgiveness comes through loud and clear. The director exposed the ways we hurt each other and shows that no past wrongdoing cannot be undone or at least washed away.

People do have an experience at the movies. Sometimes bad, sometimes good. And it is possible to have a spiritual encounter with God that you would not have otherwise. Many people who viewed *Magnolia* had such an encounter. Truth spoke to them. They wanted a dialogue, an opportunity to share their experiences and ask questions. What did it mean? How can I find meaning and purpose? For Christians, this is an opportunity to engage in that discussion and offer a dialogue that can lead people to the ultimate truth.

The problem is that *Magnolia* is rated R and offered a fair amount of bad language. Most Christians rejected the movie as another example of the foul content offered by Hollywood. Some Christians who found their way to the theater never got past the first fifteen minutes and left. Do you think we missed an opportunity for discussion? Do you want to change the world? For most Christians, in the case of *Magnolia* or *Wendy and Lucy*, we fail to see God at work. He is speaking to us. Is it possible that *Magnolia* offers more profound truth than can be found in many Sunday morning sermons?

How is this possible? Because movies are primarily stories. They offer our experiences, objects, people, and the realities of the world we live in. All of these are capable of reflecting God's glory and truth. Our experiences are nothing more than ordinary life that reveals our hopes, fears, dreams, and aspirations. People are made in the image of God and can reflect God's love and grace. The world we live in reflects God's truth and majesty. So what is the Bible or the Word of God? It is primarily a story about man without God and man's efforts to find some meaning and purpose in life.

What Hollywood offers is a reflection of the Bible. Although filmmakers may not fully understand this process, they offer a world without God, but many of their characters are on a journey to discover truth and to find their purpose and meaning in life. Both Hollywood and the Bible offer us an unedited version of life, which includes the good, the bad and the ugly. Both present the world as it is and not a world as we want to see it. To see the truth requires us to confront the ugly aspects of our lives and the world we live in.

How do films and the Bible do this? They do this through the use of language, images and ideas. The Bible uses the written Word as its source of power and authority. Hollywood uses dialogue to convey emotions, thoughts and meaning. The Bible uses images through visual storytelling. Jesus' parables are a prime example. He used complex theological concepts and turned them into visual images inside the minds of his listeners—Jesus created word pictures. Hollywood communicates primarily through visual images. Through the use of metaphors and symbolism, Hollywood is able to communicate ideas that cannot be expressed in language alone. The Bible is a book of ideas, the primary one being that man is lost without God. Not all movies created by Hollywood contain ideas, but the good ones do. All good movies are about something. These are the ones we should be searching for. They are asking questions and looking for truth. That's where you are going to find God at work.

Some Christians believe that most Hollywood movies are an offense to God because they offer language that is inappropriate or blasphemous. A few months ago, I saw a TV special on Christian television where an interviewer was searching for Christians on the streets of Hollywood. He asked people if they were Christians. They answered, yes. He asked if they went to R-rated movies. They answered yes. The next question is the classic setup. Should you be going to see movies that take the Lord's name in vain? They had a surprised look on their faces, feeling somewhat ashamed. They answered, no. Case closed. All R-rated movies are evil and contain foul language. That was the judgment according to the producers of this television program.

It never occurred to them that God could actually be at work in some of these films. The third commandment tells us not to take the name of the Lord in vain. So what is this commandment saying to us? Is this about language or something more? Who does it apply to? What constitutes a misuse or improper use of God's name? When we are transformed, we become a representation of who God is. We are his representatives; therefore, his name becomes our name. When we misrepresent him or live a life that is inconsistent with his truth, we are misusing his name or misrepresenting his nature. This commandment deals more about the bigger issue of how we live our lives than about the use of language.

Is there a clear-cut answer to whether or not you should go see a movie that contains offensive language? I believe it ultimately will be a decision between you and God. It will involve your personal relationship with God and the level of your spiritual growth. In some ways, this is a gray area, but I do believe that movies which contain bad language can reflect his truth and speak to us. This leads to a dialogue with the culture. They are asking questions and looking for someone to give them the answers. Do you think we might have some answers? We will never get to this point unless we are willing to take the journey and understand that media and entertainment presents us with an opportunity not only to make films that reflect God's truth but also to watch movies that reflect his truth. Movies can challenge us to examine the way we live our lives.

I was born in 1956, which places me in the middle of the baby boomer generation. I consider myself an early member of the church of media and entertainment. Over the years, I have realized that media has defined the person I am today. I don't believe I would have become a producer, director, writer or, for that matter, the founder of two media ministries without the influence of The Waltons and The Excorist. Perhaps, there has never been a greater contrast between two programs. But both clearly shaped the person I am today.

During the 1970s, The Waltons was one of the most successful family dramas on television. I watched it faithfully every Thursday night. I seriously doubt that I was the intended audience or demographic that the producers were aiming for. But I made a connection with The Waltons, especially the character of John Boy played by Richard Thomas. I identified with his character and his aspirations. Although we lived in different times and in different places, there were striking similarities. We were both poor with little prospects for the future. John Boy wanted to make something of his life. He wanted to be someone and go to college. I was the same age as John Boy. I could see myself in him. We were both dealing with the same struggles. I cheered for him to succeed. If he could make it, perhaps I could too. If he could dream and work hard maybe in my life anything was possible.

The Waltons and John Boy inspired me. I was not a Christian at the time; however, I believe God used this television program to give me hope for the future.

In the early 1970s as a teenager, I saw *The Exorcist* with a few of my friends. At the time, *The Exorcist* was a big hit. It was provocative and cutting edge. It was the rage, a must-see film. I wasn't sure about God. In fact, I had been to church once in my entire life. I knew nothing about the Bible. And I wasn't sure if God even existed. In other words, I was a nonbeliever. I did not have the opportunity or the good fortune to grow up in a Christian home. Call me a heathen.

But after seeing *The Exorcist*, something changed. Yes, it was the scariest movie I had ever seen in my entire life. But it was more than that. Its seemed so real. Perhaps, for the first time, I had the sense of what evil looked like, and it wasn't a pretty picture. I could actually feel its presence. It shook the very foundations of how I viewed everything in life. If the devil was real, there had to be a God, right? And if the devil had that much power, shouldn't that be something I should be concerned about? And if there was a war between God and the devil, which side did I want to be on?

That was a lot for a teenager to think about. In one sense, I felt like hell had been scared out of me. I'm not sure that's what the filmmakers intended or the message they were sending. But it was clear to me that there was a spiritual world after all. No. I didn't immediately give my life to God or convert to Christianity or, for that matter, start going to church. But it did start me on a pathway to seek the truth. And that, my friends, is the power of film. It would be another four years before I would become a Christian and a believer. But I have no doubt that it all started very innocently on a Saturday night at the age of 16 watching The Exorcist at the old Showcase Cinemas in Erlanger, Ky. It was a life-changing moment in my life.

The Waltons and The Exorcist are examples in my life of television and movies that helped change me and put me on a path toward God. Today I believe we can change the media culture and create opportunities for others in the same way that The Waltons and The Exorcist helped me as a youth to discover God.

You might ask how we can be effective using media today to change lives and make a difference. Consider this analogy. Have you ever tried to work outside in the sun on a hot summer day? Let's say a really hot summer day at 105 degrees. How productive are you? Everything is a challenge. It takes every effort just to stay cool and survive the heat. What would happen if you turned the temperature down to say 95 or 90 degrees? It would still be hot. But it would be a bit more bearable. Perhaps we would be more effective and productive in our work. What if we could get the temperature down to 85 or 80 degrees? We would no longer be hampered by our environment. We could be fully productive. The media culture is like a hot summer day at 105 degrees. It makes us ineffective. Somehow, we have to find a way to turn down the temperature. By doing so, no matter what our ministry, we will be in a better position to further the cause of Christ. The reason that ministries are not successful is because of the environment the media culture has created.

In the next few chapters, I will share five core principles that will turn our media culture crisis into an opportunity that can change our world. As bold as it sounds, we have the capability with God's help and grace to change our world. But first we must understand the forces behind today's media culture and how the perfect storm formed to create a church of media and entertainment.

The first principle presents no easy answers. It requires us to be actively involved in the process of change. That means time, effort and money. Most of us go about our daily lives unaware of the changes which are happening in our society. The future will be very different. The continued growth of the media church will make certain of that. For good or bad, its coming. Today's current generation thinks differently. They will come to see Christianity in a different light. They are more likely to see it as one of many religions that contain some truth but not a definitive truth.

Maybe we have reached a point where we believe that we can't change anything. That's true to a point. In our own power and abilities, it is impossible to change the world. But remember, God is still at work. He is working today in the media culture as you read this book. All that he requires of us is to join him in that work. This is a partnership between us and God. Philippians 4:23 says, "For I can do everything through Christ who gives me strength." *(NIV)* And Mark 11:23 says, "I tell you the truth, you can say to this mountain, 'Go fall into the sea'. And if you have no doubts in your mind and believe what you say will happen, God will do it for you." *(NIV)*

The question is, do we believe these scriptures. Does scripture have a purpose? Or are they merely words on paper? The time has come for us to believe that anything is possible because through Christ we can change our world, including the media culture. We have three choices. We can pretend there is no crisis and continue to do what we are doing and hope for the best. Or we can acknowledge the media culture crisis and hope it will just go away. Or we can acknowledge the media culture crisis and view it as an opportunity to engage the church of media and entertainment.

5   Principle 1—The Media Culture Crisis and Positive Change

I offer for your consideration five principles that I believe will change our world. They involve the combination of media, faith, and culture. They are interconnected and dependent upon one another in order to achieve results. Without accepting the first principle, you cannot move on to the second principle and so on.

Principle 1. Christianity is rapidly loosing its impact on culture. Today the media controls the culture and, by doing so, controls the hearts and minds of the people. That includes young and old, Christians and nonbelievers. It is no longer possible to determine where culture starts and where media ends. They have merged to create a media culture which, in turn, has created a media culture crisis. When we recognize how media is influencing and changing us, we will understand that our perception of media and entertainment needs to change. Then we can utilize the opportunity this crisis presents for positive change by promoting and producing media and entertainment that reflects Biblical truth.

I have been a Christian for 34 years and have served the Lord as a youth leader, a cell group leader, church media director and have engaged in evangelical outreach. In 1999, God called me to full-time media ministry, and I left the Federal Reserve Bank after 20 years of service. As founder, I spent two years establishing the ministry and serving as Executive Director and later as Director of Media and Education. I created and produced *The Zone*, a youth program that ran on Channel 9, WCPO, in Cincinnati, Ohio for 11 years. I received weekly e-mails from grateful parents and testimonies from youth whose lives had been changed.

It seems like I have always been a media guy. God showed me early in ministry that media, television and movie making could be a conduit that he could use to reach the world. I have researched and studied media and its impact on culture for years and wondered when someone would write a book putting all the pieces together.

One day as I was out on my daily run, the Holy Spirit started speaking to my heart about reaching our culture through media. Was God calling me to write this book? (I believe that if Jesus Christ would have come in our day, he would have used the most powerful and far-reaching influence in our society today—media, including television and movies.)

So every day I ran, the Holy Spirit gave me ideas. I came home and did my research. One day the Holy Spirit impressed me with the thought that God had a plan on how to change our current culture. That included raising up and training youth and young adults as missionaries to media in general and to Hollywood.

I believe we are in a media culture crisis. Even President Obama called our society today a media culture. God wants the Body of Christ to be instrumental in bringing about this change. In the Bible, we see many instances where God chose the most unlikely individuals to do his bidding and to go to a people group he wanted to reach.

Remember when Peter had the vision on his rooftop about the unclean animals. God told him to arise and eat. God was calling a Jew to reach across well-established boundaries and take the Gospel of Jesus Christ to those Peter considered to be unclean and uncircumcised. Do you think God was maybe trying to change his mindset?

Why do you think God would make a course change in how his church is doing things? It seems the world today is resistant to Christianity. Maybe we're not making that much of a difference or are missing the mark. Maybe we have also been influenced and infiltrated by the modern media to an extent we are not aware of. Instead of us changing the world, could the world be changing us in subtle ways—a little here and a little there—being slowly and strategically drawn into a web?

Some Christians argue that if we simply live out our lives and be Christ-like we can change the world. But why is this not working? Sure, we can see pockets of our faith in action. But, for the most part, our society and the world in general goes about its business as if we, the Body of Christ, do not exist. We have become irrelevant. Only two things can happen. We are advancing the cause of Christ and changing our society or Christianity is in retreat. There is no middle ground. We cannot remain static.

What Could Stand in Our Way?

Some people see the issue as too big or too complicated. So it's easier not to think about it. Some have a false sense of security choosing not to have cable TV, not watching R-rated movies, or by limiting their exposure to media in general. Others believe we can't change it even if we wanted to. For some, it's much easier to justify that it's somebody else's problem. And there are those who don't want to believe or admit that we are just as likely to be influenced and controlled by media as the general public.

Understanding the Relationship Between Media and Culture

Why do we have a media culture crisis? Because it is part of the air we breathe. It goes beyond one movie, one television program or one cable network. Media impacts every aspect of culture and society. Remember, I am referring to a *media culture crisis* **not** a media crisis. There is a substantial difference. When movies, television programs and media begin to impact our shared consciousness, it then has the ability to change our behaviors, attitudes, and actions. That includes altering our institutions, such as schools, government and the Church. It is a crisis for Christians because the influence the media is creating in culture is having a negative impact on our society, which is leading people further away from God and his truth.

How does this work? Sexuality is one of the major themes in today's media culture. In fact, 68% of all television programs offer some form of sexual content. The average

American television viewer will see 14,000 instances of sexual acts per year. Today Hollywood offers sexually-charged movies, such as the movie *American Pie*, including its following six sequels and its many spinoffs, which are primarily aimed at an adolescent audience.

Not only are television and movies sexually charged, but advertisers embrace sexuality as a means to sell products. For example, *GoDaddy.com*, whose primary business is selling domain names, uses provocative models in the process of disrobing in their commercials. They then direct the viewer to go online to see more of the action, which they brand as restricted viewing. Their form of advertising doesn't suggest their products offer better value than their competition or tell us why their service is superior. They seem to suggest that using GoDaddy.com is sexy. So how does all of this impact the average American teenager and lead us to our original question, why is there a media culture crisis?

I am sure that if media did not exist, which would include movies and television, young people would still be engaging in sexual activity. As the Bible says, there is nothing new under the sun. But when media and culture merge, that's a game changer. It can offer either a positive or a negative impact. In the case of sexuality, media or at least those who create the media have decided that it is important. They understand that sex sells. In fact it's not really about sexuality. Media makers use sexuality as a device to hold our attention. Their primary motivation is to build audience share and increase ad revenues.

Media makers identify and direct the culture to consider what is important. It's not that they tell us what to think or how to think, but the messages they choose to communicate become important by virtue of just being present in the media. When sexuality is incorporated into media, it is elevated to an important status. In other words, because it is present in the media, it becomes important. By deciding to omit or ignore topics such as a committed relationship and marriage, teen pregnancy, sexually-transmitted diseases and the emotional fallout and guilt associated with sexual activity, the media conveys the idea that this is not important and not worthy of our consideration or discussion.

This theory about how the media culture functions would suggest that talking about sexuality and casting it in a positive light would actually promote promiscuity. I believe media functions as an amplifier of the culture. As media searches out the new cultural shifts, concepts and trends, they discover that some young people are engaging in sexual activity. So they incorporate and reflect that within their media. In turn, the media acts as an amplifier to increase the strength and influence of sexual activity. The media picks up on this increase within the culture and communicates it back through its media. It is accepted in greater numbers and is, once again, picked up by the media. The process continues to repeat itself over and over. It becomes a 10-fold, 100-fold, 1,000-fold affect on increasing sexual activity or promiscuity.

To be fair, not all media supports promiscuity. Consider the film *Juno*. The lead character, Juno, is a teenager who engages in a sexual relationship that leads to an unwanted pregnancy. She makes the courageous decision of not taking the easy way out. Although pressured to have an abortion, she decides to give up the child for adoption. Although Juno contains sexual contact between two teenagers, it does not endorse the activity. In fact, it serves as a cautionary tale. Both Juno and her partner were emotionally unprepared to enter into a sexual relationship. They certainly were not prepared to face the likelihood of becoming parents before they graduated from high school.

Juno makes the case that sexual activity has consequences, which can impact lives forever. Juno goes against the grain by promoting a different message than the one that is accepted throughout mainstream media.

Having a better understanding of the relationship between media and culture helps to explain why we are in a media culture crisis. But it doesn't have to remain a crisis. The media culture in and of itself is neither negative nor positive. It is neither good nor evil. It does not suggest that all forms of media, including movies and television, are necessarily to be avoided or branded as taboo. As the creators of media, **we** decide which message to communicate, and **we** decide how we are going to use media. The media culture crisis presents an opportunity for Christians to use the crisis as a catalyst for positive change. How do we do this? By promoting and embracing media and entertainment that reflect Biblical truth. This is already taking place.

There are Christians that work in Hollywood today, who are creating art that can transform the culture. And, as difficult as it sounds, God is also using secular filmmakers to create art that reflects his glory and truth. How is this possible? God will do what he wants to do regardless of whether or not it fits into our theology. In Isaiah 10, verse 7, the Bible says, "But Assyria's king doesn't understand that I am using him; he doesn't know he is a tool for me." (*NCV*) God will fulfill his plan according to his will, not ours. I think part of his plan is for Christians to use the media culture crisis to our advantage. For example, God will use anything to get our attention, including speaking through a donkey, as in the story of Balaam.

> Numbers 22:27-31 says "When the donkey saw the angel of the Lord, she lay down under Balaam. This made him so angry that he hit her with his stick. Then the Lord made the donkey talk, and she said to Balaam, 'What have I done to make you hit me three times?'" *(NCV)*

> Balaam answered the donkey, 'You have made me look foolish! I wish I had a sword in my hand! I would kill you right now!' But the donkey said to Balaam, 'I am your very own donkey, which you have ridden for years. Have I ever done this to you before?' 'No', Balaam said. Then the LORD let Balaam see the angel of the LORD, who was standing in the road with his sword drawn. Then Balaam bowed facedown on the ground."*(NCV)*

> Verses 34-35, "Then Balaam said to the angel of the LORD, 'I have sinned; I did not know you were standing in the road to stop me. If I am wrong, I will go back.' The angel of the LORD said to Balaam, 'Go with these men, but say only what I tell you.' So Balaam went with Balak's leaders." *(NCV)*

If the media culture has been capable of creating a negative impact, then it is just as capable of creating a positive impact that can lead people back to God. I am convinced that the media culture will play a significant part in the next great revival.

How the Media Culture Has Impacted Us

God wants us to use the media, the most powerful force of our day, for the advancement of the Kingdom of God.

If we are to do this, we first must recognize how the media culture crisis has impacted Christians. I will not bore you with all of the statistics, analyses, and studies. But I do trust their results. We have more than enough information from Christian and secular outlets, such as the Rand Corporation, George Barna, the Kaiser Family Foundation, Media and the Family, the Bridger Generation and the list goes on.

What are their findings? Faith seems to have little or no impact on our lifestyle choices. Our behavior and attitudes are linked to our exposure to violence, sexuality, and media in general. The research suggests that the media culture extends beyond the reach of the electronic screens of our media devices. Consider this analogy. We are being exposed to a low form of radiation. We cannot taste it. We cannot hear it. We cannot see it. Nor do we feel its effect immediately. But over time it will kill us. And just like exposure to low radiation, exposure to media over a period of time is killing us spiritually and making us ineffective.

The Real Message the Media Culture is Communicating

Whether it's on a conscious or subconscious level, Media is sending us a clear message: *I (as an individual) am the center of my universe. I am more important than anything else. My needs, wants and desires must be met at any cost.* The message comes in the form of instant gratification and the glorification of wealth, power and sex. This helps to explain our obsession with consumerism, which is at the root of most of our problems.

Businesses and corporations want to sell you products or services. Media outlets need cash to produce programming. In turn, they are able to create content that can influence the culture. Their influence becomes desire. As desire increases in the culture, it creates demand. Demand fuels the cycle, which takes us back to square one.

The entire media culture crisis as well as its central theme (materialism, wealth and power) can be summed up from one of the most famous quotes in movie history. In the film *Wall Street*, Michael Douglas's character, Gordon Gekko, says, "The point is, ladies and gentleman, that greed, for lack of a better word, is good. Greed is right. Greed works. Greed clarifies, cuts through, and captures the essence of the evolutionary spirit. Greed, in all of its forms – greed for life, for money, for love, knowledge – has marked the upward surge of mankind, and greed – you mark my words – will not only save Teldar Paper but that other manufacturing corporation called the USA." [5] Gordon Gekko has revealed everything that is wrong with today's media culture.

Should we put our needs and wants above everything else in life? Not only has this philosophy impacted the general culture, but its greatest impact can be felt within the Church.

Some argue that today's market-driven church is a reflection of this philosophy. Have we bought into the same reasoning that Gordon Gekko believes will save his company as well as America. Bigger is better. Why are we interested in marketing and branding? Many churches today seem to be embracing this philosophy of creating products and services that meet peoples demands. Are we building a church that reflects Christ, or are we building a church that looks prestigious and powerful? Are churches just interested in making people feel comfortable?

If we follow the same model that today's media culture is built upon, which is to determine what people want and then give it to them, we will find ourselves participating in that same media culture. The media culture is creating churches that are embracing a marketing plan for growth based not on the power of Christ but on the type of experience that they can create for you. The goal is growth; therefore, you do nothing that will cost you your people. Craig Detweiler, a professor at Fuller Seminary in California, puts it this way. "The media is a process lived in the marketplace, driven by consumerism, fueled by advertising, and obtained by celebrity."[6]

We find ourselves in a similar situation as when satan tempted Eve with the DESIRE to taste the fruit. She was convinced she had to have it. Today, the media culture uses desire in the same fashion. The power of the media has pushed us onto an accelerated track that we can't seem to get off of.

Nowhere is this affect more intensified than on our youth. Today's media culture has become the "new church " for a new generation. It is a place of worship. It takes place in our local multiplexes, our mobile media devices, and on our computer screens and flat screen televisions.

Under the age of 18, the average daily consumption of media is nearly 8 hours a day. It's raising our kids. Some studies suggest that 70% of kids that are now in church youth groups will abandon their faith. I realize that this is disturbing. However, many people I talk to refuse to accept the findings. Over the past 25 years, I have worked with high school and college students and with many youth ministries. By what I've seen and heard, I'm convinced that the numbers are right on target.

Often, I am able to ask questions when kids are more relaxed and open. I have found that most young people don't know what they believe. And what they do believe, they can't tell you why they believe it. Their Christian worldview is somewhat fragmented. Parents don't want to believe that their teens fall into this category. Parents believe that by setting standards, such as no cable TV and other guidelines, they are safe. But are they? Parents and youth workers see what they want to see. Sure, everything might look good on the surface, but nobody is willing to look under the surface. To see the truth would be too unsettling, and we won't know how to respond.

I am convinced that on some level all of us have been influenced by the power of the media to believe that our wants and desires are important and must be satisfied. We are as likely to be compromised as nonbelievers. Every advertisement tells us that we must have it now and what we do have isn't good enough. This philosophy goes cross-grain to Bible teaching concerning making Jesus our Lord and

Savior. We've done a good job of making him our Savior, but it's the Lord part that we are failing at.

When we realize how important this issue is and what's at stake, we can begin to change our attitudes and views on how we perceive media and entertainment. We will then be able to take advantage of the opportunity this crisis presents for positive change. We will be able to promote and produce media and entertainment that reflects Biblical truth. If we reject Principle 1, there is really no hope or anywhere else to go. We cannot change the media culture until we realize that change starts with us. But first we need to understand the language of media.

6   Principle 2—The Language of Media

Principle 2. Christians must become media literate so that we are knowledgeable in the language of media and its influence. By doing so, we can unlock the meaning of the message that media communicates and take control of how we respond to the message.

What would it be like if we couldn't read or write? How would you use the internet? It would be impossible to get a job. In today's society, reading and writing are essential skills. Or can you imagine living in a foreign country and not knowing the language? Simple things like using the transportation system or ordering from a menu at a restaurant would be challenging.

Knowing the language is essential for navigating through life. Just as we need to be able to read and write, developing media skills is now just as important. Media has its own unique language. It consists of design, structure, meaning, and syntax. For Christians it is absolutely essential that we understand the language of media, which brings us to our second principle.

John 8:32 tells us that the truth will set us free. We need to know the truth and not just what anybody calls truth. Is what the media communicates to us really the truth? Or is it a distortion of reality? Understanding the tools and language of media will help us to be discerning. By not understanding the language of media, we are held captive to any message which the media wishes to communicate. Our goal as Christians is not to be subject to the control and influence of media.

We now live in a media culture that surrounds and envelopes every element of life. Our best defense is to become media savvy. For the most part, we don't understand what we are being exposed to. For example, we would consider a G or PG movie to be relatively safe. And we would view most R-rated movies as offensive. But in reality, the G or PG movie today could contain more anti-Christian and anti-Biblical content than the R-rated movie. In fact, the R-rated movie could be a redemptive film which embraces Biblical views. Often we make assumptions that are not based on the facts.

Most people, including Christians, consume media without processing its purpose, goals, and message. We don't ask challenging questions about its authenticity. Therefore we become sponges absorbing everything we see and hear.

How do movies or television shows or any media affect my decisions, values, and behaviors? Have you ever thought about it? Do you assume they don't affect us? Do you think it is something we should consider? These questions could be answered in a media literacy program.

What is media literacy? In the past three years, I have taught media literacy to over 100 students. Only five students had ever heard of the subject. Media literacy teaches and unlocks the language of media, which contains five elements. (1) It helps to define the message media communicates. (2) it reveals the purpose behind the message. (3) It identifies how the message impacts the individual. (4) It identifies how the message influences behaviors and shapes perceptions in society. (5) It offers resources on how we can take control of our response to the message.

We should be teaching media literacy in children's church, junior and senior high school classes, and small groups in every church in America. It is essential curriculum. Most of us have no idea what the real message is in today's media. For example, I often use *Starship Troupers* in my media literacy classes because it seems like an innocent sci-fi, action thriller. The film is set in the future with earth battling an alien species of bugs on a faraway planet. Seems harmless. Or is it?

Could the film be communicating a political message that casts doubt on our very way of life? It can even be an anti-American film. Director Paul Verhoeven weaves an interesting tale in which he believes government is misleading and lying to its citizens. They are convinced that war is good and just. But the people are being misled and are unaware of the government's true intentions. The government is only interested in their agenda. They want the natural resources of the alien planet. Some believe Verhoeven's real purpose was to criticize America's political and military objectives not only in the Middle East but globally as well. Is America becoming a new totalitarian and fascist state?

So is this innocent science fiction or political commentary? How do we know? Could this movie have an impact on your beliefs? I'm sure your first answer would be an absolute No! But what about on a deeper, subconscious level?

In Matthew 10:16, "Look, I am sending you out as sheep among wolves. So be as shrewd as snakes and harmless as doves." *(NIV)* I think a case could be made that today's wolves represent our media culture. If we are to be shrewd as snakes and harmless as doves, we need to understand media literacy. If we are going to be successful expanding the Kingdom of God, we must know what we believe and why we believe it. I don't want the media to define my truth and my beliefs.

All filmmakers, including writers, directors and producers, have a point of view (POV). In fact, we all have a POV. Some people refer to this as a worldview. Our POV defines our attitudes and core beliefs. Without a POV, we would not be able to interpret the world around us. Point of view offers a perspective and insight into how we view politics, religion, social issues and personal lifestyle choices. The POV of Paul Verhoeven, director of *Starship Troupers*, has been shaped by his life experiences. As a child, he grew up in The Netherlands, his home country, during the German occupation. He was exposed to a totalitarian and fascist regime that routinely used propaganda to proclaim Nazi superiority. It unquestionably has influenced his political and social views, which are evident in his film *Starship Troupers*. Understanding the POV helps us to unlock the message within a film, television program or media in general. By using the tools of media literacy, we become more effective in identifying the POV.

Ecclesiastes 8:1 says, "How wonderful it is to be wise, to be able to analyze and interpret things. Wisdom lights up a person's face softening its hardness." (*NLT*) Understanding the language of media is to be wise. Embracing the concepts of media literacy gives us the ability to analyze and interpret everything we see and hear. I think movies especially have the ability to challenge us to examine our life choices and lifestyles. They can be a doorway to the truth. There have been countless examples of where God has used mainstream films to touch people's lives. Media is neither evil nor good. It is a conduit that carries whatever message we choose to communicate and by whatever manner we choose to use.

So why are we not teaching media literacy? First, for most people, it simply is not on the radar screen. But if it is, we just don't understand what media literacy is. Second, there is a lack of instructors. Media literacy is a difficult subject to teach if you don't have a background in media. Third, we don't believe there is a media culture crisis. Media is no big deal. Fourth, we are not sure what our views are on media. So why get into it?

But what does a good media course consist of? First, the program must encourage people to think for themselves. When I teach media literacy, I tell my students, "I am not here to tell you what to think but to challenge you to start to think about what you see and hear in the media. You must come to your own conclusions." Second, the program should be designed to not paint Hollywood as the villain. We must be objective. Third, media literacy needs to be interactive through a multimedia presentation.

A media literacy program contains the following: (1) It starts with awareness and education. (2) In order to apply media literacy, you must develop a skill set that utilizes various techniques and strategies. In other words, it offers you a toolbox that you can use to unlock and read the multiple layers of image-based communications. (3) In order for media literacy to be successful, it must be applied daily.

The most important elements of media literacy are common sense tools, such as teaching students how filmmakers use editing to create a reality that doesn't exist, how colors can create different emotional responses, or how camera movement and angles can affect an audience's perspective.

And the most critical part is challenging students to take control of how the message is impacting them. Should I accept or reject the message? Does it reinforce my beliefs? Does it ignite my passion to live a life consistent with my Christian principles? Does it challenge me to bring positive change to my life as well as to others? Does it cause me to act on my beliefs? Does it cause me to be more socially conscious? Or do I reject the message because it is not consistent with my Christian beliefs? The more we ask ourselves challenging questions, the closer we are to discovering the truth.

Today's media culture is here to stay. It will continue to influence our society for some time to come. If you believe that there is a media culture crisis, then I am sure you would agree that it would be important to learn the language of media and to become media literate. In fact, our media culture influences every level of our society, and that includes our institutions, such as the Church, schools, government and entertainment. No aspect of our culture can escape its grasp. We cannot simply turn off the television or unplug from society. God is calling us to be good stewards of the media we consume. Our responsibility is to distinguish the truth from the untruth because both are present in our media. God can use both truth and untruth to point us to his love and glory.

Learning media literacy is equivalent to wearing a radiation suit. It allows us to live in our society without being exposed to the negative effects that can harm us. We are influenced by people around us as well as our institutions. Our exposure to the media culture not only comes from our firsthand exposure, such as movies and television programs. It also comes from secondhand exposure, such as family, friends, work associates and society in general.

If we want the world to change, it starts with us. We all have a responsibility to become media literate. By just spending 15 minutes a day studying or reading about the subject, you can start to become media literate. We are currently working on our website to be able to offer all of the resources necessary to start your journey. We have developed an extensive media literacy program, which can be taught online at mediamissionaryschool.com or in a classroom setting. I will talk more about this in a later chapter.

If you see the need for media literacy, then you have accepted Principle 2 and are ready to move on to and implement Principle 3.

7   Principle 3—Hollywood the New Mission Field

Principle 3. In order to engage our culture, we must recognize Hollywood and the entertainment industry as a legitimate mission field. In fact, Hollywood represents a unique people group or tribe that for the most part has not been reached. They have their own language, customs, and culture. In order to redeem Hollywood and the broader entertainment industry, we must stop blaming them for all of society's problems and begin a dialogue of reconciliation.

I have been a Christian since 1976. During that time, one thing that the Body of Christ has agreed upon is the need to support foreign missions. I have never heard anyone argue against financial support for missions or the need to send missionaries overseas. It is a universal concept accepted in the Church and is the basis for the Great Commission. We all know the scripture by heart. Jesus said in Acts 1:8, "But you will receive power when the Holy Spirit comes upon you. And you will be my witnesses telling people about me everywhere, in Jerusalem, throughout Judea, in Samaria and to the ends of the earth." *(NLT)*

Most of our churches actively send out short-term mission teams, who pay their own way, on a routine basis. Youth ministry also supports short-term mission trips. Students raise their own support through fundraising activities and typically will spend up to two weeks during the summer on a mission field. Whether it's through humanitarian efforts such as digging wells for clean water, building a school or an orphanage, or through evangelistic outreach, we are unified in our efforts to reach the lost in foreign lands or to the ends of the earth as Jesus commanded.

I would wholehearted agree that we need to fully support foreign missions. But we have missed something in this scripture. Remember, those that Jesus was speaking to were actually in Jerusalem. That's local missions. What Jesus was referring to was to start where they were and then to move over to the next town and then to the next region and then to the world. Think locally and then globally was the model that Jesus was communicating. In recent years, we have made a better effort embracing the local missions concept. Outside of many of our churches, we often see signs saying "You are now entering the mission field". That's a step in the right direction. However, we have a mission field that we have completely ignored that has the ability to influence the world. This brings us to our third principle.

So is Hollywood a mission field? According to Karen Covell, Director of the Hollywood Prayer Network, only 2% of media professionals go to church or synagogue. She goes on to say that Hollywood is an isolated society ignorant of and often hostile to Christianity. That would certainly qualify them as an unreached people group. People in Hollywood and the broader entertainment industry have often been described as a tribe because they have their own gods, customs, language, culture and belief systems. There are similarities in Hollywood to what we see in unreached people groups with strange customs in faraway places, such as Africa or South America. So why don't we see Hollywood as a mission field?

Hollywood is like Nineveh. Jonah was commanded by God to announce his judgment. But Jonah had animosity toward these people because they were wicked. And he refused to do what God commanded because he knew God would have mercy on them. Eventually, Jonah accepted God's will. Jonah 3:10 says, "And when God saw that they had put a stop to their evil ways, he had mercy on them and did not carry out the destruction he had threatened." Jonah 4:2 Jonah says, "That is why I ran away to Tarnish. I knew you are a merciful and compassionate God, slow to get angry and filled with unfailing love. You are eager to turn back from destroying people. Jonah 4:11 says, "But Nineveh has more than 120,000 people living in spiritual darkness, not to mention all the animals. Shouldn't I feel sorry for such a great city." Because Jonah responded to God, the people of Nineveh were saved." (NLT) To this day, Nineveh for the most part is a Christian city.

We know where God stands on the issue. Shouldn't we also show mercy for Hollywood? So why are we acting like Jonah acted and refusing to go. First, we have been at war with Hollywood for so long, we know nothing else. We have made our views known through boycotts, threats, and protests. Often it has become ugly and, quite frankly, very unchristian. Sure, the content of many of the television shows and movies produced have contained offensive and questionable material, but that doesn't justify our tactics. The fact is that many Christians simply hate the people in the entertainment industry.

Second, we blame Hollywood for polluting the minds of our youth. We see them as responsible for much of society's problems, including pornography, drug use, violence, promiscuity and promoting anti-Christian views. For many of us, we just simply cannot forgive them for what they have done or what we think they have done. It also is hard to see Hollywood as a mission field when the people there enjoy a lifestyle of the rich and famous that includes wealth, power and influence.

And, finally, Hollywood and the broader entertainment industry doesn't look like a third-world country. They don't fit into our way of thinking. We like to put our Christianity in a nice, convenient box. Hollywood doesn't fit into that box. In reality, most of the people who work and live in Hollywood and the entertainment industry are decent people like us. They are not the stars that we think they are but are everyday working people trying to raise a family, pay the mortgage and just get by. They need to be reached. For every director or movie star, there are hundreds of people behind the scenes building the sets, moving the camera gear, setting lights, running the audio, etc. They are the people of Nineveh.

If we are going to reach Hollywood and fulfill the Great Commission, we must have a different mindset and a change of heart, which starts once we embrace our first two core principles.

When we recognize that we have a media culture crisis and decide we want to respond to the crisis, we must start first with reaching Hollywood. Remember Hollywood is the most influential mission field on the planet. If we reach Hollywood, we reach the world. Consider this. Foreign missionaries will tell you that the greatest influence on their people group is the American media. Media produced by Hollywood shapes the hearts and minds of people around the globe. Some 60 years ago, the President of Indonesia requested an audience with some of the key Hollywood executives of the day. He stated that he regarded them as political radicals and revolutionaries, who had hastened political change in the East by creating unrest. He said what the Orient saw in a Hollywood movie was a world in which all of the ordinary people had cars, electric stoves, and refrigerators. Now the Orient regarded itself as an ordinary person who has been deprived of the ordinary man's birthright. If that was 60 years ago, you can only imagine how our influence has increased throughout the world.

What happens if we embrace Hollywood as a mission field? Not only do we influence the uttermost parts of the earth, but we get a 2-for-1 deal. We also can impact our own hometown and our own local mission. Why? Because Hollywood's influence is everywhere. It's the only mission field that extends beyond the physical limitations of a confined space and time. America's number one export is entertainment. If we embrace Hollywood as a mission field, our message will be part of whatever Hollywood is exporting.

By accepting Hollywood as a mission field, we are embracing Jesus' commandment found in Acts 1:8 which says, "But you will receive power when the Holy Spirit comes upon you. And you will be my witnesses telling people about me everywhere, in Jerusalem, (in your hometown), throughout Judea (in your state), in Samaria (in Hollywood) and to the ends of the earth." *(NLT)*

We have a passion and conviction that drives us as Christians in our efforts to embrace foreign missions. No sacrifice or effort is too great. We are on board with a "whatever it takes" attitude. We need that same passion and mindset if we are to be successful in our efforts to redeem Hollywood. I know we can do it. And I'm sure it's on God's "to do" list. The only question is are we willing.

When we accept Principle 3, we can move on to the fourth principle, which will give us discernment, wisdom and the help we need to fulfill Principle 3.

8   Principle 4—Praying for the Entertainment Industry

Principle 4. Prayer is the foundation of the Christian faith. Without prayer, nothing is possible. Christianity currently faces a media culture crisis. Therefore, we must pray for both Christians and nonbelievers working in Hollywood and the broader entertainment industry as well as all other media fields. We must pray for God's Kingdom to become a reality in the entertainment industry.

Throughout my years of being in the Church, including Sunday School, Sunday morning sermons, small groups and Wednesday night services, I cannot think of one instance where someone offered up a prayer for Hollywood and the entertainment industry, whether that was for Christians working in the business or for nonbelievers to come to know Christ. Quite frankly, the entire concept of praying for Hollywood has not been a priority or even on the radar screen. But if Hollywood is the most influential mission field, why aren't we praying? Prayer is the foundation of the

Christian faith. Without prayer nothing happens. We must invite God to do his work in this world (his Kingdom come, his will be done on earth as it is in heaven). I think it is safe to say that prayer is the game changer. Consider the following scriptures.

> Don't worry about anything; instead, pray about everything. Tell God what you need, and thank him for all he has done. Philippians 4:6

> Never stop praying. 1 Thess. 5:17

> Confess your sins to each other and pray for each other so that you may be healed. The earnest prayer of a righteous person has great power and produces wonderful results. James 5:16

> I also tell you this: If two of you agree here on earth concerning anything you ask, my Father in heaven will do it for you. Matthew 18:19

> You can pray for anything, and if you have faith, you will receive it. Matthew 21:22 (NLT) (all)

Matthew 21:22 tells us that we can pray for anything. That includes Hollywood, which brings us to our fourth principle. Of all of the five principles, prayer is the most important. So why didn't I make prayer the first principle? Because we won't pray for Hollywood unless we understand why we need to. And unless we accept the first principle that we are currently in a media culture crisis and that we must be part of the solution, we will not pray for Hollywood. If we won't take the time to become media literate and understand the power and influence of media, we won't pray for Hollywood. And, if we are not willing to accept Hollywood as a valid mission field and recognize it as the world's most influential mission field, we won't pray for Hollywood.

The first three principles help us to understand why we must pray for Hollywood. They give us the motivation to act and become part of the solution. Can you imagine what would happen if every Christian would start to pray for Hollywood on a daily basis? Do you think we would see a change? Can you imagine God's Spirit moving in Hollywood and throughout the entertainment industry? Can you imagine the impact of actors receiving Christ? This is not fantasy. It could happen if we make it a priority to pray. The part that every Christian can play in solving our media crisis is to pray.

So why don't we pray? And not just for Hollywood. To be honest, we really don't like praying because prayer is probably the most difficult thing to do. We sometimes approach prayer as a last resort. I'm been guilty of that. Sometimes it's hard to believe anything is going to happen. We've been praying our entire lives, and it seems like God isn't hearing us.

Some are convinced that prayer is too hard. It takes up too much time. It's impossible to get up at 4:00 a.m. and pray for two hours. Basically, we have turned prayer into a job. For some, it's a matter of fear. Or what if God actually answered our prayers? It might mean that we would be required to do something that we are uncomfortable with.

There are a myriad of ideologies out there. Here are a few of them: God is on vacation. He created the world, and now it's up to us. Some approach prayer as a last resort. We think we've got everything under control. God has given us gifts and talents so all we have to do is put them into action. So why get God involved? If we just work hard enough and smart enough, we'll get the results we want.

Concerning Hollywood, praying seems to be just a waste of time. The issue isn't all that important. It's all meaningless and harmless entertainment. Right?

In Appendix I, I talk about the history of Hollywood and how they came to be viewed as an enemy by the Catholic and Protestant churches. However, we are called to pray for our enemies? How about Luke 6:27-28 where Jesus says, "But to you who are willing to listen, I say, love your enemies! Do good to those who hate you. Bless those who curse you. Pray for those who hurt you." *(NLT)*

Without knowing all the facts or seeing the whole picture, we conclude that Hollywood is in direct conflict with Christianity. However, I believe God can change all of that if we take the initiative and pray for the people there to be changed by an encounter with Christ.

If we can agree that prayer is important and that Hollywood should be a focus of our prayers, how do we do it? Let's make it easy. You don't need to pray two hours a day for Hollywood. Can you find three to five minutes? Remember, when you pray, you are talking to God just like you talk to anyone else. You can pray anywhere and at any time. How about on your commute to work? I don't believe in making prayer complicated. Do you?

Here's an example. Pray for God's Kingdom to come and his will to be done in Hollywood as it is in heaven. Pray that Christians have favor and opportunities to witness to their fellow industry professionals. Pray that they receive discernment and wisdom on which projects they should work on. Pray for creative ideas that illustrate God's love and grace. Pray that God will raise up, equip and send media missionaries to Hollywood and the entertainment industry. Pray for nonbelievers in Hollywood to receive Christ. Pray that God's Spirit will fall upon every set and production throughout the entertainment industry.

If we prayed the above points, just think what God can do in answer to our prayers. Do you want to change the world? Do you think prayer could be the key? If so, you are on your way. Could it be this simple?

Check out HollywoodPrayerNetwork.com. To know how you can specifically pray for Hollywood, there is no better resource than The Hollywood Prayer Network. They offer I-to-I Prayer Partnerships, incognito prayer teams, and prayer walks. They also get kids involved with a kid's prayer calendar.

Most of us will never go to Hollywood to work in this business. But we can do our part by influencing Hollywood through our prayers. Everything changes when we embrace the fourth principle.

So let us Pray. Watch. And see how God will move in Hollywood. With prayer we will be able to execute our fifth and final principle.

9   Principle 5—The Rise of the Media Missionary

Principle 5. The Body of Christ must raise up, equip, train, and support media missionaries to the mission fields of Hollywood and the broader entertainment and media industry. Our purpose is to reseed the culture with mainstream entertainment and media that reflects Christian and Biblical values. We do this by partnering with the mainstream, entertainment and media industry.

If Hollywood is a mission field, then it will be necessary to send missionaries. Throughout the 19th Century, Christians reached out to the people of Asia, Africa and the South Pacific. They saw these places as mission fields that required training, development and support of missionaries. Africa is not a mission field without missionaries just like Hollywood cannot be a mission field without missionaries. So what kind of missionaries do we send to Hollywood and the entertainment industry? What is their role? Who do they work for? What is their purpose? Is it to reclaim, redeem, and transform, or is it to infiltrate the entertainment industry? Do they make Christian movies and media? The idea of Hollywood being a mission field raises many questions.

A missionary to the entertainment industry is called a "media missionary". What is a media missionary? If you ask that question to 50 Christians working in the mainstream entertainment industry in Hollywood or elsewhere, you would probably get 50 different answers. The same would be true if you posed the question to those who work in Christian film and media. The definition of a media missionary is a work-in-progress. It's an ongoing discussion we have at our ministry website mediamissionaryschool.com.

Here's our basic view of a media missionary. Without question, it is someone who is under the control of the Holy Spirit. I don't see any way you can succeed in this industry without God's direction and your willingness to allow the Holy Spirit to direct your life. So what should media missionaries be doing? Preaching the Gospel? Producing Christian films? Working in Hollywood? Telling stories?

If they should be telling stories, what kind of stories should media missionaries be telling? Jesus taught by telling stories about everyday life. His concept of communicating was the parable and is the model that media missionaries should embrace. Jesus said the Kingdom of God is "like" not that the Kingdom of God "is". Jesus embraced the power of the story. The vehicle he used to communicate was through oratory (story telling). If Jesus came today, he would, most likely, use the media.

A media missionary is someone who makes films or media that speaks of Jesus the least but has him most in mind. It is a difficult concept but one that is very profound. In order to embrace the concept, one has to see Hollywood as a partner. We will not be able to change the world or our culture without working with Hollywood.

When I talk about Hollywood, I am speaking about not just the physical place but the entire media and entertainment industry. Should we be working with Hollywood? I Corinthians 9:21-22 says, "When I am with the Gentiles, who do not have the Jewish law, I fit in with them as much as I can. In this way, I gain their confidence and bring them to Christ. But I do not discard the law of God. I obey the law of Christ. When I am with those who are oppressed, I share their oppression so that I might bring them to Christ. Yes, I try to find common ground with everyone so that I might bring them to Christ." *(NLT)*

Because of Hollywood's influence throughout the world, they are the most important mission field of our day. Yes, we should be partnering with Hollywood. A media missionary is someone who wishes to redeem and reform Hollywood. That doesn't mean leaving Tracs on the set or impressing people with our spiritual language and phrases. In order to reach nonbelievers in the entertainment industry, the media missionary must be Christ-like, living out his or her values, morals and Biblical worldview with integrity in front of his or her peers.

Being a media missionary is not about infiltration or subversion. We are not in the business of propaganda. If we want to be effective, we will tell stories that are honest, broken and, above all, true. So the goal is to work in the mainstream entertainment and media industry. That can be in Hollywood or elsewhere. The media missionary's purpose is to make movies and media for a mainstream audience or general audience that reflect Biblical truth. Here are some examples of films where I see the media missionary at work: *Bella*, *The Spitfire Grill*, *Lars and the Real Girl*, and *To End All Wars*.

How do we develop and train media missionaries? Currently, there is no training center or program. There is no school dedicated to the development of the media missionary. Our goal at mediamisionaryschool.com is to create resources that will lead to the development of media missionaries. It is a first step in the right direction.

Why is it important that they are equipped and trained? Christian ministries based in Hollywood report that many people are coming to Hollywood claiming to be missionaries. Most of them have no training, have no concept of what a media missionary is, lack the giftings and talents necessary, don't understand what they are getting into, and lack a plan. You get the picture. It's a mess. Perhaps, some of them are actually called to be there. But they lack the resources and knowledge to be successful.

Hollywood and the entertainment industry is a hard business. Over 90% of those who go to Hollywood will not make it through their first year. The odds are against them. That's why we need a training program that will determine if they have been called to Hollywood and if they have the talents and giftings necessary to navigate through the treacherous minefields that they will undoubtedly encounter. In fact, many Christians working in Hollywood could use a similar training program.

It's quite possible that many who think they are media missionaries are not. And some Christians in Hollywood who don't consider themselves to be media missionaries could very well be so called. So why are Christian colleges and universities who have film and media programs missing the mark? Because their goal is not to develop media missionaries. Their goal is to teach you to write a script or direct a movie, or learn how to use a camera, etc. They instruct you in your core competencies so you can graduate.

Yes, some schools do offer classes in film and theology. However, they are not practical applications because they are based more in the theoretical concept of God and cinema. Over the years, I have talked to many students at various Christian colleges, and I get the sense that they do not understand the concept, mission and purpose of a media missionary. Their main mission is to get a job.

Training a Media Missionary is a Four-step Process.

Step 1 is **To Raise Up**, which is the process wherein you determine if you are called by God to be a media missionary. First, You have to examine whether or not you have been called and what your purpose is.

A few years ago, I took a course called *Experiencing God, Knowing and Doing the Will of God* written by Henry T. Blackaby and Claude V. King. It offered a process by which we can understand the will of God. Often we ask what God's will is for my life. For example, "Am I called to be a media missionary", and "Should I go to Hollywood?" But the real question is, "What is God's will and where is he at work?" God is at work everywhere, including every human activity. That also includes Hollywood and the entertainment industry.

If we are going to know God's will, we must have a relationship with God. It has to be real and personal. We must know his character, his motives, and his purposes. It's only then that we understand what we believe and why we believe it. He will then invite us to join him in his work. God will speak by the Holy Spirit through his Word, prayer, circumstances and the Body of Christ to reveal his purposes and his ways. It is during this phase that we start to realize what our calling actually is. God's calling will always lead us to a crisis of belief that requires faith and action.

Next, we have to decide if we want to make the adjustments in our lives to join God in what he is doing, not in what we want to do. That may mean going to Hollywood or accepting the fact that we are not called to be a media missionary. It's at that point that we truly experience God by obeying him. He then accomplishes his work through us.

Second, check your motives. Do you want to serve God or serve your own self-interests. Just because you have a love and passion for film and media doesn't mean you have been called to be a media missionary. Having a desire to be rich and famous is not a good indication that you have been called. Right motives go a long way in determining your calling. Finding God's will is dependent on a life focused on God and his activity and the ability to deny one's self as well as be humble before God.

Third, you have a vision for Hollywood and the entertainment industry. Can you love the people in this business? Why do you want to go to Hollywood? Sure, making movies is fun. But are you ready to serve people? A media missionary first and foremost is a servant. You are there to love people into the Kingdom of God. Can you love people that don't agree with you, those who don't share your values and morals, or those who may consider Christianity a joke?

Fourth, do you really understand the role and purpose of a media missionary? This takes time and work. A lot of people think they understand what a media missionary is. There are many Christians working in Hollywood and the entertainment industry who do not function as media missionaries. To be a media missionary requires a unique skill set and a profound understanding of your role and purpose.

Consider the following scriptures: Galatians 1:15—But God had special plans for me and set me apart for his work even before I was born. Romans 11:29—God never changes his mind about people he calls and the things he gives them. Isaiah 49:1—Before I was born, the Lord called me to serve him. The Lord named me while I was still in my mother's womb. Hebrews 5:4-5—To be a high priest is an honor, but no one chooses himself for this work. He must be called by God as Aaron was. So also Christ did not chose himself to have the honor a being a high priest, but God chose him. Romans 12:2—Do not be shaped by this world; instead be changed within by a new way of thinking. Then you will be able to decide what God wants for you; you will know what is good and pleasing to him and what is perfect. (NCV) (all)

Media missionaries need support, especially during this first critical phase. Often parents, family members, friends and the Body of Christ can squash these dreams and hopes. If someone came to the Body of Christ and proclaimed that he/she has been called into the ministry or to the mission field, I can't imagine that it would be met with criticism and doubt. Most likely they would receive support and encouragement. Shouldn't we do the same for media missionaries? Isn't their calling just as important?

Why so much opposition? Some can't understand how you can be successful as a media missionary. The concept doesn't make sense. God doesn't call us to be successful but to be obedient. Some see Hollywood as an evil place. They are afraid that those we send as media missionaries will be contaminated by the dark side. But when you think about it, satan entices young people to run with the crowd who get into alcohol and drugs, etc. on the home front as well. That's why it is so important to have a day-to-day dialogue and walk with God. As with anyone, it is a daily choice to listen to the Lord and follow where he leads. There are ministries in Hollywood that can connect you to a community of believers who can help support and encourage you. And what about the power of God that works within us to accomplish the calling and keep us safe? Doesn't that work in Hollywood as well.

From a practical point of view, we will need to consider how we will make a living. Some parents I have talked to would rather see their kids get a degree that leads to a more stable and predictable career path. But that violates the entire spiritual perspective of a calling. Serving God has never been practical. However, with the right training and equipping, we can increase the likelihood of them getting a job. Also, remember those whom God calls he also equips.

I believe that parents, friends, and the Body of Christ would be more supportive of media missionaries if we had a training program. This would allow people to explore their calling in a safe environment before going to the mission field. In many cases, students may very well discover that they have not been called. For those who have been called, we will be able to focus on their development and training.

Step 2 is **Equip**. This is the process where you develop and gain an understanding of your spiritual gifts and talents. First, what are your talents and gifts? We all have been given spiritual gifts. If you have been called by God to be a media missionary, he will have given you the talent necessary to complete the task. You cannot create talent. It can be enhanced, but it either is there or not. But what about talent? Are you a writer, director, producer, actor, etc? Each discipline requires a completely different skill set. And what spiritual gifts have you been given? Discernment? Wisdom? Knowledge? They all will be required.

The Formula

Mediamissionaryschool.com has created a formula to help predict your success in the entertainment and media field. Here's the formula. $T + (N + K + E) + (C + A + D + F) + P + X = TP$.

T is for talent worth 50 points. It is a determining factor, but you can have talent and still not succeed. Talent is one of those things that you either have or you don't. It is absolutely a God-given gift. You cannot go to film school and develop talent. If you are born to be a director, you will be a director. If you are born to be a writer, you will be a writer, etc. The fact is most of your instructors in film school will know after a short time if you have what it takes to make it. The only question is whether or not they will be honest with you.

So let's say you want to direct. Can you make it in the business with marginal talent? Absolutely. But it will require you to be stronger in other areas to compensate. It might also mean that you would be better suited to be a first or second assistant director.

N is for networking worth 40 points. The media business is all about networking. It's really who you know that is going to help you to work in this business. People like to work with people they like and trust. So how do you network? First, you need good social skills along with an excellent understanding of how the industry functions. Both are essential to be a good networker.

Do you know how to work a room? It's without a doubt an art form. It certainly helps to be friendly and likable. You create an environment where people respond to you because you make them feel good, and they just like to be around you. It's also essential to be a good communicator. It's important that you be interesting and capable of telling a good story. Perhaps the most important factor is being capable of listening to people. In other words, you care more about what they are saying than what you have to say.

Networking should always lead to relationship. And relationship will lead to trust and opportunities. Think of networking as your chance to help other people first. With whom do you network? Start with your own peers at film school, conferences, workshops, etc. When you are networking with people in higher positions, find out what they need and whether you have something you can leverage to meet that need.

K is for knowledge worth 40 points. Obviously, you need to know everything about your field. If you plan on being an editor or cinematographer, develop your craft. This is not only about a four-year experience you have in college, but it must be a lifetime commitment. The more you know, the more you will understand. And the more you can put into practice will dramatically increase your chances for success in whatever media field you choose. Read everything about your field. Find mentors who are experienced and knowledgeable and will show you the practical side of how to apply your craft. What you don't know will kill you. In this business, people will know in the short term whether you are knowledgeable and know what you are talking about. You will not be able to fool people. Knowing the language of how people communicate in this industry is essential.

E is for entrepreneurship worth 40 points. Let's stop fooling ourselves. Opportunities usually don't come looking for you. Do you really think someone is going to offer you a $30 million picture to direct right out of film school? Especially in today's economic environment, you can't afford to sit around and wait for the phone to ring. Entrepreneurs make their own breaks and create their own opportunities. They are people who see things that other people don't see.

Opportunities are everywhere. That's how an entrepreneur thinks. For example, I just met a young filmmaker starting out in Hollywood. He has worked on several films as a production assistant. It's entry level work. But he saw an opportunity that others didn't see. He wrote a pamphlet called *The PA Guide, A Practical Guide to Your First Job in Film or Television* by Shannon D. Roddy. As far as I know, there has never been a specific book written on the topic of the production assistant. This met a need in the marketplace. The fact is if you don't know how to be a good production assistant, do you think you will get an opportunity to move up? It's an excellent resource because it tells you everything you need to know to be the best production assistant you can be. He is selling the book for $7.95. This is a classic example of an entrepreneur in action.

What does it take to be an entrepreneur? A good study of people, solid communication skills, and a solid grasp of business principles are all essential ingredients. Most people who get to direct, produce or write their films, work in the independent model. That means you have to self-finance your projects. Entrepreneurs know how to raise money, make deals, find distributors and return a profit to the investors.

No you don't have to be good at being an entrepreneur to make it in the media business, but it sure helps. If you are weak in this area as well as mediocre in talent, you are probably out of the running.

C is for confidence worth 20 points. Can you project confidence? Not false confidence. Obviously, your confidence should come from God and not your evaluation of your talents and skills. In this industry, perception is reality. If you are not confident about yourself being a filmmaker, others will not take you seriously. If God has called you to work in media and entertainment, then exert your confidence. Remember the famous line as it applies to producers: "I have several projects in various levels of development." This can be an absolutely true statement as long as there's a few thoughts in your head or perhaps a few things written down. The point is do you have the confidence to sell it.

A is for attitude worth 20 points. The wrong attitude will sink your career. Nobody wants to work with difficult people. I have hired a lot of crew members over my career. I can forgive a lot of things. But I will not bring somebody back who has a bad attitude. That's like throwing gasoline on a fire because it can spread throughout your crew. The media, film and television business is no different than any other aspect of life. It's all about the right attitude. Are you willing to serve others and start at the bottom? If you have a servant's heart, you will have the right attitude to make it in this business. Are you good at making adjustments and adapting to difficult situations? Your attitude will be the determining factor.

D is for drive worth 20 points. Can you outwork everybody else? The media business requires long hours and dedication. If you are looking for a 40-hour week job, you have chosen the wrong career. A couple of years ago, I worked with an intern who was a fourth year media student. Her plan was to be a television journalist. The problem was she discovered in order to do that she would be required to work long hours including weekends. She wanted her Friday and Saturday nights off to go out with her friends. Do you think she found a job in her field as an anchor or reporter? If you are not ready for long hours and working weekends, change your major now. In the film business, a typical day can be 14 – 16 hours. Remember, the advantage you have is your youth. The question is do you want it bad enough.

F is for focus worth 20 points. Can you be laser-like in your approach to your work? Seeing the goal at hand is the secret of focus. In the media business, there are all types of distractions. For example, you can start believing all your own hype that you are special or that the rules don't apply to you. That can lead to bad lifestyle choices as well as to the people you hang around with. All of this is a distraction and will cause you to loose your focus. You can find a lot of successful, talented people who no longer work in the film or television industry because they lost their focus.

P is for a plan worth 15 points. Have a plan. Then have a backup plan. And then again have a second backup plan because in this business things change fast. You get the point. You have to have a plan. Preferably a good one. Writing a plan in and of itself makes you think about the process. You become an active participant in your career and not merely a bystander. And, frankly, people will be more impressed with you if you have taken the time and effort to actually develop and write a plan for your own professional and personal development.

X is the unknown factor worth 40 points. The X factor will mean different things to different people. Some people call it fate, chance, coincidence, dumb luck or destiny. For Christians, this is God's plan and purpose for your life. After all of your hard work and effort, it will probably be the X factor that will determine whether or not you actually make it in this business. For some of you, this may be hard to fathom. All of the other elements get you close to the finish line. It's the X factor that takes you across the line.

Obviously, the X factor works in your favor if you've been called to be a media missionary. But it's not guaranteed. You must do your part so God can do his part. That means you have to work on your attitude, your confidence, your drive and your focus. You've studied hard and are knowledgeable in your craft. When you have done all this, the X factor kicks in on your behalf. On the other hand, if you are just trying to coast in, don't expect the X factor to do much for you.

TP is for total points. When you add up all the factors, what number do you need? Remember this is only a theoretical calculation with a possible 305 points. You need to be over 200 points. I consider between 200 and 220 to be marginal. In fact, anything over 220 would put you more in the safe zone.

So how did I make the evaluation? For example, talent is worth 50 points. With any score under 17 or below, it's not happening. Between 18 and 35 is marginal or average. For 36 and above, you are showing visible signs of talent in some area, such as directing skills, writing, producing or acting.

So where do you stand? If you've done the work, attained your degree and really applied yourself, chances are you have one true talent that you excel in. That would put you in the upper half of the top third. You probably have three or four categories that you are somewhat efficient in. You would score in the lower end of the top third. You also have three or four categories in which you are adequate or average. That would put you in the lower or the middle end of the middle third. And most students have one category in which they have serious problems. In this case, you would score in the lower third. The trick is not to score in the lower part of the bottom third. When you add it all up, for most students, you are within striking distance, but it is often the X factor that will determine whether or not you make it.

Now ask yourself if you have what it takes to make it in this business. What do you have to work on and improve? More importantly, what are your strengths? Remember, you don't have to be good in every factor, just excel in what you are good at.

The Importance of the Holy Spirit

The X factor is the Holy Spirit at work in your life. In order for the Holy Spirit to be effective, we must allow the Holy Spirit to control and lead us. Without the direction of the Holy Spirit, it is impossible to be a media missionary. John 14:26 tells us that whatever we need, the Holy Spirit will supply. The media missionary's work is a spiritual calling. Acts 1:8 tells us that after we receive the Holy Spirit, we will have power. You will not be able to do this in your own strength. God may very well have given you the talent, but you will need the spiritual gifts to fulfill the calling.

I Peter 4:10-11 says, "God has given each of you a gift from his great variety of spiritual gifts. Use them well to serve one another. Do you have the gift of speaking? Then speak as though God himself were speaking through you. Do you have the gift of helping others? Do it with all the strength and energy that God supplies. Then everything you do will bring glory to God through Jesus Christ." *(NLT)*

Romans 12:6-8 says, "God has given us different gifts for doing certain things well. So if God has given you the ability to prophesy, speak out with as much faith as God has given you; if your gift is that of serving others, serve them well; if you are a teacher, teach well; if your gift is to encourage others, be encouraging; if it is giving, give generously; if God has given you leadership ability, take the responsibility seriously; if you have a gift for showing kindness to others, do it gladly." (NLT)

Jesus says in John 16:13-14, "When the Spirit of Truth comes, he will guide you into all Truth. He will not speak of his own but will tell you what he has heard. He will tell you about the future. He will bring me glory by telling you whatever He receives from me." (NLT)

So what are some of the gifts of a film and media maker? We can find our inspiration in the Bible. We are teachers, servants, encouragers, and leaders. And we do this with compassion and love.

NOTE: It's vital especially during Step 2 for students to have a mentor. Nothing is more important than having a committed Christian who is a media professional to personally advise and disciple a potential media missionary.

Step 3 is **Training.** This is the process wherein you receive the knowledge and training that you most likely would not receive in film school or college.

Do you understand Christian and Biblical worldviews? Without them, you cannot be a media missionary. Can you recognize other major worldviews, such as secular humanist, post-modernism, cosmic humanism or new age?

How is God at work in Hollywood? This involves understanding how theology and film intersect. I'm not interested in theory. We need practical application on how to incorporate Biblical principles into mainstream Hollywood. That's not as difficult as it sounds.

God is at work in Hollywood. And he has used secular filmmakers to tell his stories. For example, we can find God's fingerprint in movies such as *Lars and the Real Girl*, *Juno*, *Places in the Heart*, *Bella*, *Signs*, *Magnolia*, and *Grand Canyon*. What makes these movies spiritual? Can we discover the patterns? These are the lessons that the media missionary must learn.

One thing students will not learn in film school or, for that matter, even in a Christian college or university setting is Media Literacy. It is essential for future media missionaries to understand how media literacy works.

Hollywood is a business. That's why they call it show business. Film schools don't do a good job of teaching the basics on how the industry functions. The following are some examples. How are projects financed? How do you buy film stock? What do things really cost? What goes on in deal making? What are the essentials of distribution? How does the marketing of a film affect its success? How do you network?

What filmmakers should know is what they are often not taught. For example, most film schools teach students the "studio system" as if they were going to graduate college and start making $30 million films for a major studio. That's unlikely to happen. Christians who are called to be media missionaries should take note that their best opportunities may be to enter into low-budget or independent filmmaking. A media missionary program will teach the skills necessary for low-budget filmmaking.

Christians who are coming to Hollywood need access to resources that will help them live and function in the industry. Where is your spiritual support system? Without one, you could be overwhelmed by the industry. Learning where the resources are is critical. You will need a church and fellowship group, as well as practical answers to where you can find affordable housing. You should know these answers **before** you go.

Here are some of the basic questions that students often ask. How do I function in the entertainment industry as a media missionary so that I can complete my calling? In a practical sense, what projects should I be working on? What roles should I accept or reject? How do I function as a Christian in this business? What is my responsibility as a Christian in this industry? These questions get to the heart of the role and purpose of a media missionary.

Seven Christian Groups Working in the Industry

The above questions have created confusion for those who are passionate about their faith and their love for media. How do the two work together? In order to make sense of our calling, sometimes we look for predictable patterns or a framework in which we can work. It helps to explain how things work and what God is expecting us to do. But, in reality, it may or may not be his will.

I have identified seven groups of Christians that work in the entertainment and media industry, some within the Hollywood or the studio system and others outside of the system. None of the groups are right or wrong. But it would be a mistake to think that God works only in one group and not in the others.

In my opinion, God can use any form of media to touch audiences. But I feel that perhaps the seventh group, The Media Missionary Group, expresses God's overall vision and passion for art and the people who make it.

Group 1. Full Message Group

This group consists of Christians who predominately make evangelical films. For them the message is more important than viewing filmmaking or media making as an art form. They usually have a laundry list that needs to be checked off, which usually includes a full representation of the Gospel message and spiritual laws. Undoubtedly, a conversion scene will be portrayed at some point in the film. Most people in this group work outside of the Hollywood system.

There is a subgroup I call "Full Message Light". Although the message is still important, they do believe that the entertainment value of the film has some merit. They are also not as likely to be as dogmatic in the need to check off every item on their laundry list.

Group 2. Conquerors

This group views media in a militaristic way and believes they are at war. Their goal is to infiltrate and conquer Hollywood for Christ. Their strategy can best be summed up as a Trojan horse approach. By entering Hollywood, they can inject mainstream movies with Christian values. In doing so, they can take over Hollywood from within. The problem with the Conquerors is that they don't view Hollywood as a partner; therefore, they are unlikely to be employed for any length of time. Their rigid philosophical approach to filmmaking and their moral convictions make it difficult for them to relate to anybody in Hollywood. Most likely they are forced back to the Full Message Group.

Group 3. Positive Values Group

This group loves movies and believes in the power of media. They believe that entertainment, first and foremost, should be innocent and harmless. They create positive and uplifting entertainment that reflects family values. No darkness is allowed within their films, television programs or media in general. They are primarily interested in producing G or PG films.

Group 4. Positive Values with an Edge

This group supports many of the principles of the Positive Values Group. But they aim their material at a slightly older audience. They are willing to look at more complex moral issues as well as explore the human condition. They may on occasion support some R-rated movies, such as Schindler's List and Shawshank Redemption. But, for the most part, they do not venture beyond the PG-13 rating.

Group 5. The Under-the-Radar Group

This group wants to create non-evangelical, mainstream movies with some level of understated Christian content. The problem is that often the Christian content is just an add-on. It lacks a purpose or a justification for its existence. It feels like the writer is manipulating characters and plot points just for the purpose of injecting some Christian message. This group wants to work with Hollywood, but their primary motivation is not to the art form but to the message. They see the art form as a necessary means to an end. What we are left with is an unrealistic view of life.

Group 6. The Quality Circle Group

This is the most difficult group to understand. They see that their primarily responsibility and duty as Christians is to create films and media that reflect quality and excellence. They also believe that their work must be marketable. They embrace moral integrity that treats people with love, honesty, and respect. They also believe that your moral integrity demands that you must serve your employer first and not seek to subvert your employer with hidden Christian motives.

I absolutely agree that Christians must embrace excellence; however, there is something missing that this group doesn't recognize. A media missionary has more than just a responsibility to his/her employer and the media business in general. There is a spiritual component at play which is the will of God and what he wants to do in Hollywood. It's not an either/or proposition. You can have integrity, believe in excellence, and create marketable work for your employer while also serving a greater purpose.

Group 7. Media Missionary Group

A media missionary must seek a greater purpose. I am sure most Christians have worked in each of these groups and at times have moved back and forth from one group to another. Are they fulfilling their calling as media missionaries? On some level perhaps. But I believe there is another group that goes beyond these six groups. In some ways, it is like entering a fourth dimension. I call it the Media Missionary Group. There are very few in this group, and most may not recognize that they are part of it.

The Media Missionary Group is under the control and direction of the Holy Spirit. Their faith defines who they are as a person, not their filmmaking or media making. They are motivated by something more than what they want. They recognize God at work and join him in that work. Their work in essence becomes an act of worship to the Lord; therefore, their responsibility and calling is to serve him through their art. Sounds easy. Right? Not really. It comes with years of experience, wisdom and knowledge.

Becoming a media missionary is a long journey. At some point, you are no longer pursuing projects that you believe will reflect Christian values, but those projects start to pursue you. I call it the fourth dimension because it is entering into a supernatural, spiritual realm. This is a place that will be different for every person. What this looks like will be between you and the Holy Spirit. Without his supernatural influence, favor and enabling, your role as a media missionary is like walking a high wire that can be dangerous and full of pitfalls. When you enter into the Media Missionary Group, you are not concerned with genre, rating, or how marketable the project is. You stop thinking about it. The main reason why we fail in the role of a media missionary is because we are trying to do the work and make the decisions in our own power. The media missionary has no agenda except to do the will of God. Ultimately, it will not be what we think it should look like.

Step 4 is **Support.** This is where the Body of Christ must provide the support system necessary to encourage, uplift and provide financial resources when needed. Many have been called and are ready to go. I'm sure they don't fully understand the role and purpose of a media missionary, but they are ready to begin the journey. They need our support. Without it, they will probably fail. First, they need their family behind them. A supportive word of encouragement can go a long way. They need to know that their family members believe in them. What they don't need is to be ridiculed because they want to go into the entertainment industry as a media missionary. All of us need to realize that in the culture we live in, God is creating new avenues and opportunities for ministry.

It is extremely important for the Church to embrace and support media missionaries. The Body of Christ can be the difference maker. Being called to be a media missionary is as important as being called to be a teacher or pastor. We have never lived in a culture as complex and media driven as today. God wants to prepare a group of people as missionaries who are uniquely trained and have an understanding of how God can work to point today's and future generations to him.

Media missionaries need financial support, especially during the first two years. Hollywood and the entertainment industry is a tough business to break into. Most fail because they do not have the initial support necessary to survive the first two years. A media missionary's best strategy is to raise financial support before going into the industry. The home church can serve as a base of operation. Individual members of the Body of Christ could offer support for as little as $20 a month. The home church can support the media missionary by providing financial resources. Other groups in Hollywood already use this strategy. They have a message they want to get out. So they support future filmmakers as well as fund projects that support their agenda. Is it working? Absolutely.

Neal Gabler in his book, *Life The Movie*, views the American culture as if it has taken on the characteristics of a movie. We have all embraced show business as if we are playing a role and long for our moment of celebrity. He argues that it is not politics or economics but entertainment that "is arguably the most persuasive, powerful, and intrusive force of our time, a force so overwhelming that it has finally metastasized into life."[7]

This is from a secular writer. So if art has become life, and life has become art, why are we, as the Body of Christ, not recognizing this and responding? Don't you think we need media missionaries?

I have laid out a strategy and a plan. Currently, only a few of those who have been called are making it all the way into the entertainment industry as media missionaries. Most are failing for an assortment of reasons. We will increase the number of media missionaries if we decide to raise them up, equip them, train them and support them. Until then, it's a hit or miss approach.

The Five Principles

Principle 1. Christianity is rapidly loosing its impact on culture. Today the media controls the culture and, by doing so, controls the hearts and minds of the people. That includes young and old, Christians and nonbelievers. It is no longer possible to determine where culture starts and where media ends. They have merged to create a media culture which, in turn, has created a media culture crisis. When we recognize how media is influencing and changing us, we will understand that our perception of media and entertainment needs to change. Then we can utilize the opportunity this crisis presents for positive change by promoting and producing media and entertainment that reflects Biblical truth.

Principle 2. Christians must become media literate so that we are knowledgeable in the language of media and its influence. By doing so, we can unlock the meaning of the message which media communicates and take control of how we respond to the message.

Principle 3. In order to engage our culture, we must recognize Hollywood and the entertainment industry as a legitimate mission field. In fact, Hollywood represents a unique people group or tribe that for the most part has not been reached. They have their own language, customs, and culture. In order to redeem Hollywood and the broader entertainment industry, we must stop blaming them for all of society's problems and begin a dialogue of reconciliation.

Principle 4. Prayer is the foundation of the Christian faith. Without prayer, nothing is possible. Christianity currently faces a media culture crisis. Therefore, we must pray for both Christians and nonbelievers working in Hollywood and the broader entertainment industry as well as all other media fields. We must pray for God's Kingdom to become a reality in the entertainment industry.

Principle 5. The Body of Christ must raise up, equip, train, and support media missionaries to the mission fields of Hollywood and the broader entertainment and media industry. Our purpose is to reseed the culture with mainstream entertainment and media that reflects Christian and Biblical values. We do this by partnering with the mainstream, entertainment and media industry.

10   Embracing a Missional Lifestyle

One of the major topics here at Media Missionary School is the purpose and role of Christians who work in mainstream entertainment in Hollywood. What type of project should I work on? How do I reach my co-workers? How do I survive in a difficult and sometimes hostile environment? These are the questions that Christians who earn a living in the entertainment business ask each day. But is it any different, for example, as anyone would face in the workplace? If you are a plumber, electrician, banker, or teacher, isn't it the same situation?

I realize that Hollywood and the entertainment industry is unique in one sense because it is the world's most influential mission field. The artists who made and produced *Gone With the Wind* in 1939 are no longer living. But their work continues and will influence generations to come. That's what makes Hollywood so unique. But what it shares in common with every occupation is in one form or another its a mission field to those who work in it. We are to approach everything we do in life as a mission field. We are called to reach the world wherever we are planted by living a missional lifestyle. It's no different in Hollywood as it is on Main Street. But most Christians have forgotten this concept. They see the mission field as something that happens in a far away country but not in their back yard. So how do you and I and those in Hollywood embrace a mission's approach to the way we live our lives? I see it as a five-step process.

1.   You must earn the right to talk about Jesus. Why is it that we think we can save people by just preaching at them and telling them what is wrong with their lives? That doesn't work in our culture. Step one requires us to realize it's not our responsibility to save people. What we are required to do is to allow the Holy Spirit to control us. By doing this, God can work through us. It's God who does the saving. How do you earn the right? You earn the right to speak into other people's lives by loving and accepting people where they are and praying for them.

2.   Be the person who you say you are. Whether you tell people you are a Christian or not, when you live and base your life on Christian principles you will be different. The people around you will see there is something unique about the way you handle yourself and your actions. In other words, you will demonstrate a spirit that is radically different than the world's. It will be expressed in your talk, your actions, and your reactions. But, on the other hand, if your life is not consistent with what Jesus taught, how do you think people are perceiving you? Is that the kind of faith and beliefs people want to embrace? Probably not. You must be the person you say you are to establish credibility.

3.   Put your faith in action. Faith without action means nothing. It's a nice story but that's all it is. As Christians, we are required to be the hands and feet of Christ. If you want to live missionally, that means you will have to go out of your way and inconvenience yourself to help people. That means effort and time. Sure people will take advantage of you, but Jesus said to turn the other cheek, love and forgive.

4.   Develop relationships. You can't make someone be your friend. All you can do is be available and open. But if you have followed the first three steps, chances are you have put yourself in a position of trust. It's amazing how many stories I have heard about Christians who work in Hollywood who talk about how people seek them out and confide in them for help and advice. These people are living missionally. They have answers. And, trust me, people are hurting. And, if they see someone whose life and relationships are working, they want to know why. Frankly, none of this is that complicated. What's complicated is living it day by day.

5.   Build friendships. If you have reached this point, friendships start to happen. All you need to do is cultivate and encourage the friendship to grow. Consider doing something together. If you are married, perhaps have your co-worker and his or her spouse over for dinner. Go to a ball game or on a hiking trip. The key is to spend some time together and just allow the friendship to grow. Now you are in a place where you have earned the right to talk about Jesus. Chances are people will be willing to hear what you have to say. After all, you have proven to be authentic and

real about your faith. You are not some slogan on a $20 fake bill with a cheesy Gospel pitch for salvation.

Final Thoughts.

If we want to change society, our culture or the world, all we have to do is embrace a missions lifestyle approach to the way we view life. I guarantee you the change won't be subtle. It will be radical. It's what Jesus called us to do in the Great Commission. He gave us the keys to how we can change our world. The question remains—are we willing to apply them. The five steps to living a missional life is a great place to start if we are serious about embracing Jesus' teachings.

Why are we not living missionally? I think there are three types of Christians that are having a difficult time applying the concepts of a missional lifestyle. The first type is what I call drive-by Christians. It seems that today Americans want their Christianity to be comfortable, safe and convenient. In other words, they don't want to get out of the car. If they do, it means getting involved in the lives of other people, and that could get messy.

The second type are the non-culturally relevant Christians. I know that in some circles the term "culturally relevant" is almost a dirty word, but over the past few years we have created a subculture that is cut off from the mainstream culture. As a result, a lot of young people today do not know how to conduct themselves or how to have a conversation with nonbelievers. They have nothing in common nor do they understand the culture or the language of today's media culture. If missionaries who plan on going to the foreign field will take two years to study the culture and the language of their people group, how can we expect to reach our culture if we don't understand it ourselves? And if we live in a Christian subculture, how are we going to relate to people in the mainstream culture?

The third type is the on-the-fence Christians. They live life with one foot in the Body of Christ and the other one in the world. To live missionally means we have to be different and stand apart. That's the only way we can show the contrast. Unfortunately, this third group of Christians are a little too close to the culture. Nonbelievers need to see something different in how we live our lives. The more Christ-like we become, the more others will be drawn to us.

Christians who do embrace a missional lifestyle are a rare group. When you embrace the five steps, you allow yourself to be lead by the Holy Spirit. It is then that God can use you to draw people to him. It becomes a matter of balance and properly ordering your life to fit into God's plan. This five-step process will work anywhere, including Hollywood, the school you attend, your workplace or your family and friends because they are all a mission field.

11   Turning Down the Temperature

Are you ready to turn down the temperature? We have presented five core principles, which I believe can and will change our world. But real change starts when we as Christians embrace a new approach and a new way of thinking on how we view Hollywood and the media. Let's consider this new approach as if it were a Hollywood movie.

We can compare our five core principles to the hero's journey. All stories have structure of which the hero's journey is one of the most commonly found in Hollywood films. You have seen it countless times. That's why most movies seem familiar. If you've seen *Star Wars*, *Lord of the Rings* or *Raiders of the Lost Ark*, you've seen the hero's journey. It consists of 12 elements that are similar to our five core principles.

The first element is The Ordinary World where the audience meets the hero, which in this case is you. The Ordinary World is everyday life. It's the routine, mundane aspects of life. It's where we are comfortable, content and pretty much doing our own thing.

The second element is <u>The Call to Adventure</u>. The hero is challenged to undertake a quest or solve a problem. Our call to adventure is to solve the media culture crisis. The first principle challenges the very concept of the Ordinary World. If we accept the call, we are no longer safe and will be required to take action. If Christianity is loosing its impact on culture and, as a result, media controls the hearts and minds of the people, that is a frightening prospect for us.

The third element is <u>Refusal of the Call</u>. Our hero hesitates or expresses fear to undertake the quest or solve the problem. We have the same reaction. The media culture crisis is too overwhelming and will require too much effort. We feel inadequate to answer the challenge. Or we deny the problem exists. We have no interest in leaving the Ordinary World.

The fourth element is <u>Meeting with the Mentor</u>. The hero, realizing that he cannot escape the truth, contacts some source of reassurance, experience or wisdom. This is the part of the story where you are looking for answers. Perhaps, you go to our website, <u>mediamissionaryschool.com</u>, searching for more information.

The fifth element is <u>Crossing the Threshold</u>. After the hero seeks wisdom, he then commits to the adventure and enters the Special World. This is the part of the story where you decide it's time to learn the language of media. You have decided to leave the comfort of the Ordinary World and seek the truth. You have embraced our second principle. Your goal is to become media literate and understand how the media works.

The sixth element is <u>Test Allies and Enemies</u>. Our hero will face situations and will discover what is special about the Special World, which in our case is the media. This is the part of the story where we learn the message media communicates or the secrets behind the media. As we encounter more information along our journey, we will also learn how we must respond to the message. We will have allies who will assist us on our journey as well as those who will tell us our efforts are in vain.

The seventh element is <u>The Approach</u>. Our hero prepares for a central battle or confrontation with the forces of failure. Our "approach" is how we view Hollywood. Is it a mission field? The confrontation will be with ourselves. If we fail to understand that Hollywood is a mission field, we will fail.

The eighth element is <u>The Ordeal</u> and is the central crisis of our story where the hero faces his or her greatest fear. Are we prepared to change the way we think about Hollywood and the entertainment industry? Are we willing to forgive past offences? For some of us, Hollywood has been a convenient target. Will we allow our animosity to drive us? That is the key question in our ordeal.

The ninth element is <u>The Reward</u>, the moment in which the hero is reborn in some sense and enjoys the benefits of the Special World. Have we reached the point where we are willing to forgive past wrongs and embrace Hollywood? By doing so, we are ready to embrace earnest prayer for Hollywood and the entertainment industry. We are free from our past. Our story has taken a turn. We now see the power of media and it's ability to do good.

The tenth element is <u>The Road Back</u>. The hero commits to finishing the adventure. At this part in our adventure, we now know what we must do. We've met our fears, and we have battled ourselves. We are ready to embrace our fifth principle. We realize we must send missionaries into Hollywood and the entertainment industry in order to complete our journey.

The eleventh element is <u>The Resurrection</u>, the climactic test that purifies, redeems and transforms the hero on the threshold of home. We are now fully committed to the cause. In our case, we need to raise up, equip, train and support media missionaries. If we are successful in accomplishing this, it will change everything, but we will have to face the test. Are we willing to do the hard work, change our priorities, redirect resources and commit our youth to the mission field of Hollywood?

The twelfth element is <u>Return with the Elixir</u>. The hero comes home and shares what has been gained on the quest, which benefits friends, family, community and the world. We have embraced our five-core principles, and it has changed us. We are prepared to share our knowledge with those around us. Because we have been changed, everything will be changed. Order has been restored to the universe, and the Ordinary World has been transformed forever.

So why haven't we embraced the five core principles? And why are we not on our own personal Hero's Journey? Those are complicated questions. I have been asking God those questions for a very long time. Perhaps, he has given me an answer. Until now, nobody has assembled the pieces in a manner that explains the problem along with the solution. For the first time we have a complete story. Our five core principles form a comprehensive picture.

The other issue that God has revealed to me over the years involves the fragmented nature of the Body of Christ. We have many groups of Christians who represent many diverse mindsets. Not only is our theology different, but also our philosophical, cultural and generational attitudes affect how we view and practice our faith. Let's take an honest look at where we are.

The Living Life Group. For them it's hard to hear anything. Life is too busy. They go to church on Sunday. Perhaps they are part of a small group and maybe occasionally are involved in an acts of kindness or outreach on a Saturday morning. But life is hard. Just getting up, going to work, and taking care of the kids is a major challenge. They can't see the big picture.

I Agree, But Group. They do agree with some elements of the five core principles. But they believe there are more important things that Christians should be doing. Typically, this group is heavily involved in their own ministry or their own church. They fail to understand how the various elements of the Body of Christ must function together.

Spiritual Group. They are heavily involved in prayer, fasting, and intercession. They go to every conference and read the latest Christian books published. They believe that if you pray hard enough, God's Spirit will move. But they are weak in the part of the Bible that talks about putting your faith into action. They fail to understand there is a partnership between you and God. And, perhaps by initiating prayer, God will invite us to join him in his work, which could require us to employ the five core principles. Maybe that's how revival will break out for our generation.

Faith-in-Action Group. They believe that if we live out our lives in a Christ-like manner we will change the world. This group is heavily involved in social action, acts of kindness, and community outreach. Unfortunately, not enough of us are doing this. As a result, we are not changing the world. Today we are finding more secular groups embracing community outreach and humanitarian efforts. Even the atheists say that you can be good without God. This group at times can overlook the spiritual element because they are more focused on works.

I Really Don't Care Group. They won't admit this, but their faith really doesn't matter. They have bought into the world's system and are quite content. They are the ultimate consumers.

I Don't Think the Media is the Problem Group. They see media as harmless entertainment that's just not that important. So the five core principles are a waste of time.

Hollywood is Evil Group. They don't embrace the five core principles because in their world it is impossible to even consider a partnership with Hollywood. Hollywood is a dark and evil place which must be avoided.

We Can't Change Anything Group. It's up to God to change the world, not us. The problem is too big, especially the media culture crisis. Essentially, this group has just given up and is waiting to die.

It's Not My Calling Group. Perhaps, this is not your calling to be a media missionary. But I believe everybody has a part in solving the media culture crisis. I think it is safe to say that we have all been called to pray. If we have a media culture crisis, why would God not want you to pray for Hollywood and the entertainment industry at the very least? We all have a responsibility to understand the power of media. I don't believe that's optional.

This is How God Works Group. People in this group have it all figured out. They totally understand how God works and functions. So the entire idea of the five core principles doesn't fit into this convenient box of how they view God.

If you are prepared to take the Hero's Journey and embrace the five core principles, I am convinced that you don't have everything figured out and are looking for answers. You are always looking for where God is at work, and you are willing to join him. You look to the Holy Spirit for your direction and guidance, and you listen for God's voice. You have struck a balance between spirituality and faith in action. You are able to connect spiritual principles to practical application.

12   Working Locally but Thinking Globally

The part you play will be decisive in carrying out and implementing the five core principles. You probably think there's nothing you can do or offer. But think again. You don't need a film degree or any experience in helping to make a difference. There are things you can do today that require little or no resources that can make a big difference in the lives of young people in your church or community. It's just a matter of getting started and taking a few small steps toward a greater goal. If we want to change the entertainment and media industry and our culture, our best strategy is to work locally but think globally.

In the following pages is a plan that you can use to start to make a difference.

What can you do in the first 7 days?

- Each day read the five core principles and commit to 5 to 30 minutes of prayer. Ask God for wisdom and discernment concerning the five core principles. Ask God to reveal his plan for Hollywood and the entertainment industry. Pray that God will give you a vision for media. Keep a log of all the ideas God gives you.

What can you do in the next 30 days?

- Commit to praying for Hollywood and the entertainment industry every day. Remember you can keep it simple by praying any where at any time. Just a few minutes is a start.
- Read The Perfect Storm, God at Work in Hollywood, and Media Literacy on our website, mediamissionaryschool.com, and start your journey to becoming media literate.
- Read my daily feature stories on the website, mediamissionaryschool.com.
- Watch a few films that illustrate Christian themes. I recommend *Bella*, *Lars and the Real Girl*, and *The Spitfire Grill*. You can also read reviews on our website and check out our study guides.

What can you do within the next six months?

- Start a prayer group that prays for Hollywood and the entertainment industry. This can be done in your home without getting your home church involved. Just invite a few friends over. Also HollywoodPrayerNetwork.com can be a great resource for current prayer requests

- Start a film night. You can do it at home or in your church. We have a list of film recommendations on our website. Most people love movies. It's a great way to start a discussion. We will provide the study guides. Just screen the film, ask a few questions and see what happens. It is a great way to have a dialogue with friends and family who don't go to church. It can be a lot of fun and a great social outreach with spiritual benefits.

- Start a dialogue with your church about the five core principles. You have influence and can be "boots on the ground". Does your church see Hollywood as a mission field? Is anybody praying for Hollywood? Has your church ever raised up media missionaries? Is your church providing financial support to any media ministry or media missionaries? These are questions that you can put on the table. The discussion starts with you.

- Commit to learning everything you can regarding the media. Our website will provide resources, books and other websites for you to check out.

- Seek out Christians in your church who work in the media in your hometown. They could work for the local TV station or production companies. See if they would be interested in coming to your film night to speak to your group. Perhaps, they may be interested in joining your prayer group. Take initiative and get them involved.

- Take it upon yourself to find young people who have a passion for Christ as well as for film and media making in your church. Talk to your youth pastor about how they are helping and supporting these young people. Are they encouraging or guiding them in the pursuit of their passion? If you have a media ministry at your church, are they involved? You would be surprised that most churches that have an extensive media program do not have high school students involved. Encourage them to mentor the youth.

What can you do in the first year?

- Start a mentor program in your church. Connect Christian media professionals with students who have a passion for film, media and Christ. This may take work and involve some red tape, but will be well worth the effort. If we are going to change anything, we have to take ownership. You can be the first.
- Personally provide financial support to a media missionary or a media ministry.
- Invite a representative to come to your church and talk about media issues as they relate to faith and culture. See mediamissionaryschool.com. We can present the five core principles to any size group.
- Maybe God has called you to be a media missionary, but you are not sure what to do. Media Missionary School provides an 8 – 10 week training program. It

will be offered online and in Cincinnati in the near future. It could be the first step for you on your journey to become a media missionary.

What can you do within the first two years?

- Work with your church to develop a media literacy program. It's not as hard as you think. We can provide training, resources and materials.
- Offer a summer film camp for high school students. You will need to work with some media professionals in your hometown. By now you should have a contact base. Mediamissionaryschool.com will help with training, resources and materials.
- By now, your church may be ready to financially support media missionaries or media ministries. But get the people on the missions board involved in the media program and encourage them to take the course on media literacy. Make them aware of the need. If you have a potential media missionary in your church, the missions board needs to know this. Make sure they get all the information and resources first before you ask for finances.

What can you do within three to five years?

- If you are at this point, you are ready to take the ultimate step. We want to duplicate our ministry. You can establish your own school for media missionaries. There is a need to have training programs across the entire country. That's why we need you.

How do you get started?

I suggest starting with an after-school media club to be held on your church campus. The program would meet weekly from 4:00 p.m. to 6:00 p.m. or from 5:00 p.m. to 7:00 p.m., whichever works best. The first hour could concentrate on mandatory training both from a spiritual and a practical application. Spiritual Application includes Finding One's Calling, The Role of the Media Missionary, Mission's Lifestyle, Worldviews, Media Literacy, etc. Practical Application includes hands-on training in camera operations, cinematography, writing, editing, lighting, etc.

The second hour could concentrate on projects. Students can create feature stories and documentaries on any ministry occurring in the church. There are stories to be found around every corner. For example, what's happening in small groups, outreach, and youth ministry that would be of interest to the congregation. Club members could work on videos that would support sermon topics. They can serve as a visual aid to support the pastor's message. There is no shortage of possible interview subjects. Everyone has a story. Who are the people making a difference in ministry and the community? Perhaps, club members could create a television broadcast for local cable access or for the internet.

You will need the following: (1) You must have support and a vision. Without the support of the church leadership and the congregation, a ministry of this type will never get off the ground. There must be a goal, an end game, and a purpose why the church will be willing to spend the necessary resources to create an after-school media club. I'm convinced that the vision must be more about the future than the present. This is an investment in changing the culture by creating future media missionaries. The payoff could be years in the making. This requires a big vision. (2) You need at least four or five students who are considering and pursuing a possible career in the media. This will be your core group. Once the program is up and running, I guarantee you that it will draw the interest of more potential participants. (3) You will need equipment. You will have to purchase cameras, audio equipment, lighting gear, and editing equipment. The cost will run somewhere between $7,500 and $25,000. (4) You will need a leader. I suggest finding someone who is a media professional. This person is crucial to your success. Not only is it important that this individual is artistically and technically proficient, but your leader must also be spiritually-minded and have an understanding of the media missionary concept. (5) Find a space dedicated to the club. Students need their own place. It tells them what they are doing is important and that they have a role to play.

Media Missionary School will assist you in developing your own unique program or after-school media club and provide all the curriculum and training necessary to get you started. We will also train your leader. We realize it can be challenging to find a media professional who will commit his/her time and efforts. You may want to start with someone on your staff who will probably have little or no experience in the media. We can provide a week-long media boot camp to get this person up and running.

13   The Future of Christianity and the Impact Media Plays

Christianity seems to be in retreat in every aspect of our culture today. In many ways, we have insulated ourselves from the world, which has lead to the creation of a Christian subculture. Many will argue that we no longer have a place in the public square and that we've lost our ability to communicate and dialogue with those who do not believe the same things that we do.

In light of the seeming retreat of Christianity in our culture today, we who care about our Christian faith need to consider what Christianity in America will look like over the next 40 years and how we can change the face of how our faith is perceived by the culture. But first, we must understand what has shaped Christianity in the post-modern era that we find ourselves in today.

George Barna, a well-known researcher, has been studying cultural trends as it relates to Christianity since 1984. His recent study conducted among 16 to 29 year olds shows that a new generation is emerging that is more skeptical of and resistant to Christianity than of people of the same age just a decade ago.

Barna's new study confirms the findings of Thomas S. Rainer in his book, *The Bridger Generation*, published in the late 1990s. Rainer studied four generations that helped to define the culture of the 20th Century. What he found is alarming. Seventy-one million people born between 1984 and 2002, roughly 1/3 of the U.S. population labeled as Generation Y is projected to overwhelmingly reject a Biblically-based worldview. Rainer also states that only 4% of this age group will embrace a Biblical worldview that puts Christ in the center of their lives.[8]

Statistics show that morals and values have been on the decline for years. What has fueled the moral decline? Our culture is facing mass problems, such as abortion, disunity in the body of Christ, consumerism, the decline of the family, and the teaching of evolution in American schools. Without a doubt, whatever issue is causing the moral decline in America, it is fueled by the mass media which includes television, movies, the internet, and news.

By the age of six, the average American child will have spent more time watching television than he or she will spend speaking to his or her parents in an entire lifetime. More than 6 hours a day are spent watching movies, television or videos. Dick Rofle, Head of the Dove Foundation (which identifies movies and videos meeting family standards) states, "When you spend that much time watching something, you have just developed new role models and a new window on life. And I think that's the destructive value of some TV and movies.... Viewers get the wrong impression and a distorted view of what life is really like."[9]

Recently, the cable television industry sponsored a study that was conducted by Media Scope. In their findings, Media Scope stated that society reflects the values of film and TV programs.[10]

George Barna has been quoted, "Young people's belief system is the product of the mass media." [11] Barna also conducted a landmark 2004 study which offered surprising results about the connection of faith and lifestyle choices. His findings have led him to conclude that faith seems to have little or no impact on one's lifestyle choices, including so-called born-again Christians. Could this be a direct impact of media and its influence, not only on the culture, but on Christians as well? Most experts agree that we have entered into a post-modern and post-Christian society. What started this transition, and how can the Church have a better understanding of cultural relevancy?

To begin with, the Church needs to break out of its Christian subculture. We have Christianized everything. For example, in the late 1970s, Christian recording artists started signing with emerging Christian record companies, which launched a new era of contemporary Christian music. Subsequently, this has lead to the creation of an entirely new industry and subculture. Up to this time, recording artists who were Christians released their material on mainstream labels, such as Capital and RCA. Their music was bought by Christians and nonChristians alike. The lyrics weren't watered down for a secular audience. The message they were presenting in their music was a Biblical view on life. Early artists who pre-dated the rise of contemporary Christian music had a significantly greater impact because they had access to a broader audience. The creation of the new contemporary Christian industry ended all of that.

Next, we need to understand the concept of cultural relevance and how we become culturally relevant to the people we are trying to reach. We need to recognize who they are, what their needs are, and how to identify with their lifestyle. We have moved from a "one dominant" culture to a "multicultural" society—from Western influence to Eastern influence, from a low-tech society to a high-tech society, from communicating primarily with words/books to communicating through images/film, and from a Christian worldview to a society with many world views, including Eastern religion, New Age, and secular. The Church is trying to communicate with the world in a language few understand today because the vast majority of the current generation has no point-of-reference in relating to Christian faith.

How can we start a dialogue with a culture that has become foreign and resistant to Christian concepts? We need a strategy. We can apply the concepts presented in the parable recorded in Matthew 13:3-23. It is the story of a farmer who scatters seed among the fields. Jesus talks about seed falling on many places that fail to take root, but in verse 8, some of the seeds fall on fertile soil that produces a crop that is 60 to 100 times what has been planted.

A harvest does not magically appear. It requires preparation and strategic planning. It must be put in the right soil, one that is broken up and moist so that it will grow. It must also be nurtured and watered before it will produce a harvest.

We are throwing seeds in many places with little or no return. The key to reaching this generation for Christ is determining what fertile soil is. Today's fertile soil is the media, and it can be used to reseed the culture with a Biblical message. The media can only be part of the solution, along with many other things, including the power of prayer, unity in the Body of Christ, and racial reconciliation, as well as teaching that emphasizes the Bible as the source of all truth.

What we do in the next ten years will affect what Christianity and society will look like in America for the remainder of the 21st Century. Christianity has always been a moving target. God's Word never changes. God is the same yesterday, today and forever. But Christianity has evolved over the centuries. It has constantly been a work-in-progress. Christians have therefore interpreted the Bible differently for each generation according to the current cultural perspective. Today's media culture presents a unique challenge to the Christian faith. No one can accurately predict what Christianity may look like in the next 20 or 50 years. A significant amount of truth has been added back to the faith over the last couple of centuries. We believe Christ is the only way to obtain salvation and that salvation is only available through grace. Is it possible these teachings could be lost again to future generations?

The market-driven church and the emergent church, along with the media culture, is changing the face of Christianity. If we don't respond and maximize our opportunities to reach out to this current generation, we could very well see a different Gospel preached in the future. Perhaps it will be one in which there are many pathways to heaven. The Ten Commandments could become the Ten

Suggestions. Other religions may be elevated to the same level as Christianity. We could very well teach a philosophy that all religions are equal and contain the same truth that will lead all of us to a transcendent heaven. We must act fast. Our window of opportunity is closing.

The battleground will be the media. Whatever direction the media culture ultimately points to will be the determining factor in how our current generation will view Christianity. That's why we have no choice but to enter into this arena. As difficult as this may sound, in the future, God's truth and glory may reside in the media culture and not in the Church itself. This could provide a refuge for a remnant of the God's truth.

The media culture presents unique challenges to the future of Christianity. But it also has given us an incredible opportunity to reach out to a new generation who live and breathe in today's media church. How do we maximize our opportunities? How do we meet the challenges? And what's our best strategies? With an uncertain future, one thing is clear. We must make certain that our message is pure.

Romans 10:9 says "If you confess with your mouth that Jesus is Lord and believe in your heart that God raised him from the dead, you will be saved. For it is by believing in your heart that you are made right with God, and it is by confessing with your mouth that you are saved." *(NLT)* Jesus said in John 14:6 "I am the way, the truth and the life. No one can come to the Father except through me." *(NLT)*

The media culture has exerted an enormous amount of pressure on the fundamental teachings of Christianity. Members of the church of media are searching for spirituality and are likely to see Christ as one of the answers but not the ultimate one. We must be clear. Christ is the only way. There is no second option. All roads do not lead to heaven.

The emergent church and the market-driven church are both examples of how the media culture has impacted the Body of Christ. If we put our interests and wants ahead of God's purpose and plan, we will fail. The media culture teaches us that we are more important and can decide for ourselves what is in our best interest. It would be easy to accept philosophies and beliefs that suggest that whatever we believe or whatever God we embrace would lead us to the truth. We must reject this. Elements of the emergent church have elevated other religions and beliefs to the level of authority of Christianity. We must reject this. The market-driven church is teaching us that it's our happiness and well being that are important and that as long as we feel good about ourselves, there is nothing to be concerned about. We must see through these strategies. God alone and not ourselves is to be at the center of our lives.

Some may say this does not express a tolerant view; nevertheless, it is the truth. We must not compromise with the media culture on the basic teaching of the Gospel message. I am also convinced the media culture is more than willing to talk. Members of the church of media desire discussion and interaction. I believe our media missionaries should be creating art that is asking questions that are aimed particularly at the members of the church of media.

As the Body of Christ, we don't have all the answers. It would be refreshing and perhaps a more honest approach if we just admitted that we can't explain everything in the Bible. The Bible does contain mysteries that simply are beyond the grasp of the human mind. John 21:25 says "Jesus also did many other things. If they were all written down, I suppose the whole world could not contain the books that would be written." *NCV* That would seem to suggest there is a great deal of knowledge that for whatever reason God has decided not to reveal. I am convinced that the church of media would welcome such a fresh approach. There is nothing wrong with sitting down and talking and discussing the Word of God, as long as we are clear that there are some fundamental truths that are absolutely essential to the Christian faith.

We must do a better job of telling our stories. Let's face it. The media culture tells stories that are interesting, intriguing, exciting, and full of drama, passion and energy. In contrast, the way we tell our stories are boring and lifeless. We have removed the mystery and intrigue from our storytelling. That's not what Jesus intended. In Matthew 13:34-35 the scripture says, "Jesus used stories to tell all these things to the people. This is as the prophet said: I will speak using stories; I will tell things that have been secret since the world was made". *(NCV)* Jesus was a master storyteller. He is our model for how we should tell stories to the media culture and the church of media. Everybody loves a good story. One thing I think we can all agree on is that Jesus was not boring. His stories were full of mystery and intrigue. He never told a story as if he were teaching a five-point sermon. He was wise and understood the audience had to participate in the storytelling process because the message contained in the story would only be truth if they came to that realization themselves.

George Miller, a renowned filmmaker, said in an interview in 1998 that organized religion had removed much of the poetry, mystery and mysticism out of our religious belief. This caused people to look for answers to their questions about spirituality in other places. He considers the cinema to be today's new place where people gather and worship as they once did in church. Miller also believes that the cinema storytellers have now become the new priests. I agree. Christians can find common ground with the church of media because we both embrace the power of stories. Eighty percent of the Bible is told in the form of a story. The media culture crisis becomes an opportunity when we realize we need to tell stories just as Jesus did by making them artful, authentic, mysterious and intriguing. Our media missionaries must reflect this viewpoint because the future of Christianity may depend on it. Stories from the Bible make the best stories because they contain the truth.[12]

The church of media seeks a common language and lifestyle. Media missionaries need to reflect what a true Christian community looks like. We have failed in this effort. So what is a Christian community and how does it function? Acts 2:44 says "All the believers were together and shared everything. They would sell their land and the things they owned and then divide the money and give it to anyone who needed it. The believers met together in the temple every day. They ate together in their homes, happy to share their food with happy hearts." And Acts 4:32 says "The group of believers were united in their hearts and spirit. All those in the group acted as though their private property belonged to everyone in the group. In fact they shared everything." *(NCV)*

So what went wrong? Does the Body of Christ as we know it today sound anything like this? One of the reasons why the church of media is so appealing is because it offers community and common beliefs. Our faith is scattered in a thousand pieces. We have no unity. Christians in the first century were of one heart and one mind. They were not playing at Christianity. They lived their faith by a common lifestyle and exhibited love, forgiveness, generosity, and respect for others. As long as we are continually influenced by the media culture, the Body of Christ will never come into full unity and reflect the true nature of a Christian community. Why? Because we will put our wants before the needs of the community. Not only have individual Christians committed this offence but also the church itself in some ways has become more important than the Kingdom of God and those Christ came to save.

One of our best opportunities today is to create art that reflects the divine in everyday life. The church of media is looking for an authentic experience. Can they find one in the Christian faith that occurs every moment of our life? John 4:23 says "And the time is coming when the true worshippers will worship the Father in spirit and in truth, and the time is here already. You see, the Father too is actively seeking such people to worship him." *(NCV)* Our experience in God is not limited to a few songs on Sunday morning. If we are to worship him in spirit and in truth, that means everything we do in life is an act of worship to God. If the church of media is looking for something authentic, this is it—a God that is everywhere. And everything we do is an expression of our love for him. This extends beyond a belief system or religion, it becomes a way of life. It transcends the physical to the spiritual.

Most Christians worship God as if he were not a spirit. Our experiences are limited to a physical place and time. You cannot take spirituality out of the Christian faith and expect there to be any truth left. No divide exists between the sacred and the secular because there is no secular world. We live in a world where most Christians leave church on Sunday morning and enter into a completely different life. For them there are two worlds, one place to worship a physical God and a second place to worship a media culture that allows us to pursue our wants. Unfortunately, many churches do not discourage this approach because it would cause people to find a more convenient place of worship where they can pursue their interests and wants ahead of God.

Our lives should not be defined by our experiences nor by our media choices. Media missionaries must create art and truth that is defined by a relationship with God. There is no authentic experience in life outside of knowing a living God. John 14:21 says "Those who know my commands and obey them are the ones who love me, and my Father will love those who love me. I will love them and show myself to them." *(NCV)* To experience God is to love God. How do we love God? By fulfilling the main two commandments that Jesus talked about. Our experiences are based on the premise of putting God at the center of our lives. Everything else revolves around God's plan. Our wants are no longer our main priority in life.

The second commandment that Jesus spoke of is to love our fellow man as we love ourselves. Again, the priority is not what we want but is to serve those around us. If we follow these commandments, we will experience God because the scripture says that God will reveal himself. 2

Chronicles says in verse 15:2 "...whenever you seek him, you will find him...." *(NLT)* We will know him by having a personal and intimate relationship with Jesus. The church of media and our current generation are searching for an authentic experience that is real, valid, and worth living for. It exists only in a relationship with God. The Body of Christ must find a way to communicate this message to the media culture.

Experiences in knowing God are not limited to a physical building or a worship service. We can know God anywhere because he is constantly revealing his presence in every aspect of life. That's how God speaks to us through movies, television programs or other forms of media. Dr. Paul L. Cox, an ordained Baptist pastor and co-director of Aslan's Place, said in his book, Heaven Trek, that he and a few friends went to see *Star Trek*. During the movie, he felt waves of the power of God come over him. Later he realized that the Lord was speaking to him in a dramatic way. The theme of *Star Trek* is *daring to boldly go where no man has gone before*. Cox felt that the Lord was asking him if he dared to go where God wanted him to go?[13] This is an example of how people can have a profound experience with God at the movies.

If you are earnestly looking for God, he will reveal himself to you. God uses whatever means it will take to get to your heart.

God is at work in the world. Our experience with God can occur at any time of the day. He will choose whatever means he desires to speak to us whether it be through people, places, nature, objects, etc. I believe the media church can better understand a God that they can experience in whatever way God choices to reveal himself.

We have limited God and made him fit into our framework. This helps to explain why many in the church of media can have a profound spiritual experience watching media because God is speaking to them though it. We must be open to how God chooses to speak to people. God works differently with each generation.

Members of the media church have grown up in a world unlike anything we have ever seen. They are a product of the media culture and have learned to pursue their wants and to put their interests at the center of their lives. Media missionaries will be used by God to reveal truth in a way that they can understand. The future of Christianity and media will be interconnected and dependent on each other. We have an enormous opportunity ahead of us.

Let's complete Jesus' plan for establishing the Kingdom of God in the media culture as well as the church of media by following his Word in Matthew 28:18, "I have been given complete authority in heaven and on earth. Therefore, go and make disciples of all the nations, baptizing them in the name of the Father and the Son and the Holy Spirit. Teach these new disciples to obey all my commandments I have given you. And be sure of this, I am with you always even to the end of the age." *(NLT)*

14   The Journey

NOTE: We are all on a journey. Perhaps you see yourself as a media missionary or someone who is concerned about the direction of our culture. Or maybe you are trying to grow in your faith in God. No matter where you are, a journey down the old road can be helpful in revealing what God wants for all of us. In fact, I'm not sure any of us can be a media missionary until we take the journey on the old road. This trip is essential in understanding the five core principles that can help us to change our media culture.

The Old Road

Welcome to the journey! It's amazing the older you get, the less you know about how God really works. I've been a Christian for 34 years and have been in ministry for over 25 years. I started a media ministry in 1987 and went into full-time ministry 12 years ago. When you think you have nothing new to learn, that's when you are in real trouble.

God has me on a personal journey to discover his nature, character and personality. It's time to re-evaluate everything. You would think that after being a Christian for as long as I have there would be nothing new to discover. But you would be wrong. As I go through this process, he wants me to talk about this journey and to be open, honest and transparent. I'm sure this is a journey we can all take. At some point in our lives, we are all going to ask who is this God we serve and what is his plan.

Part of my journey is about writing *The Red Pill, The Cure for Today's Mass Media Culture*, a book which has been inspired by the Holy Spirit. In all my time as a Christian, I have never been more certain that I have heard from God concerning the truth that he has revealed to me through the process of writing this book. I look forward to sharing it with you in the weeks ahead.

I have no plan other than to see where God is at work and join him in that effort. So I asked God each day, what should I be writing about. As I went out on my daily run, he showed me that my passion and love for the open road is a metaphor and a guide for my journey to discover how God works in our lives. I have driven across the country over 20 times. Most people think I'm crazy. I have been on practically every remote or off-the-beaten-path highway you can imagine. I particularly have an interest in Old Route 66. It is the ultimate old highway. It has been called The Mother Road. Amazingly, much of it is still intact, but it is not easy to find or follow. It requires dedication and determination. In many ways it parallels our walk with God. You have to work at it in order to follow the path.

I'm convinced that God can be found out there on the old road. Don't look for him on the interstate. Why do I like the old road? You never know what's around the next corner. There's always something new and different. I find it to be mysterious, magical and often a spiritual journey. Each curve offers a different view. Perhaps the next diner will be the ultimate dining experience. Or what new fascinating roadside attractions could be lurking around the next dip or corner? The open road offers a sense of adventure and excitement. Nothing is more thrilling than getting up early in the morning, checking your map, getting your first cup of coffee and hitting the pavement. As the sun comes up, there is a sense of uncertainty and excitement in the air. Who knows what the day will bring. There is no other experience quite like it.

Perhaps our journey with God should be just like this. So why do I think God is out there on the old road? In life we are always offered a choice. We have free will. If you want to, you can live your life on the interstate, or you can travel the back roads. It's always our choice. The interstate offers a predictable experience. No matter where you are, whether in Florida or Michigan, all interstates are basically the same. It's a very easy place to become complacent and indifferent. If you have been on one interstate, you've been on every interstate.

But the old highway is different. There is nothing predictable about it. Each road is different. It has its own course, direction and flow. You have to pay attention because the road has many curves, dips and corners. You cannot put God in a box on the old road. But on the interstate, we are convinced that God is predictable.

While the old road offers no conveniences. At any time, you may be caught behind slow-moving traffic. Who knows? The next town could be 50 miles ahead with no rest stops. The interstate is all convenience. We know exactly when and where the next rest stop, town or interchange will be. It's also fast and efficient. The interstate gives us a sense of control and allows us to make our plans and meet our goals and objectives.

The old highway is anything but that. Here you have to slow down and take your time. However, this is the key to see where God is at work. How do you see God when you're moving at 70 or 75 miles per hour when you have your own plans and goals to meet? The old road offers no convenience.

The interstate is also comfortable. It has smooth pavement. If you have been on the back roads, especially Route 66, you know it's anything but smooth. In fact, the pavement is broken and has been patched up. I think that's a good representation of our lives as we grow in our faith. God wants us to continue to grow, and it only happens when we encounter life's bumps and dips. Can you really encounter God on a smooth surface? Did God really call us to a life of convenience?

The old road also follows the contour of the land. It zigzags across the landscapes as if it's always been there. It fits into the image of the land. The interstate is anything but that. We have recreated the landscape to fit into the needs of the interstate. We have removed mountains, hillsides and valleys and have created elevated bridges to remake the land to fit into our plans. It's not hard to see God out on the old road where the road flows naturally around rivers, valleys and mountains. On the interstate, we can make God into an image we are comfortable with. On the old road, we have to fit into what God has done and is doing as we flow with the natural landscape of the road.

The interstate is also safe. It is a divided highway with wide lanes. It represents technology and the advancement of man. But you can have a false sense of safety because the interstate has a lot of traffic and people on it moving in the same direction. It becomes easier to convince yourself that this is the right way to go. Driving the interstate requires little effort. But you can be lulled to sleep and become unaware of danger. The old road is anything but safe. It has oncoming traffic, blind curves and accessible side roads. The old road requires you to be alert and prepared for anything. When driving late at night on a desolate highway in the middle of nowhere with the next town miles ahead, it is just you and God. Is our journey with God supposed to be safe and without dangers? If everything is safe, why would we need God? Are we supposed to be on the edge depending on him to protect us? A journey on the old road requires trusting in God for our protection and provision.

The old highway is connected to the land, the people, and the places that it visits and occupies. It's a place where you can feel alive. On the old highway you are more aware of the presence of God. There you will find real people with real stories. In contrast, the interstate offers a disconnected experience. There's a sense of viewing life without ever experiencing it.

And, finally, the interstate is about a destination—getting somewhere, fulfilling a goal or objective. The old road is more about the journey. It's about how you have grown in your faith and what you learn and experience along the way. The old road allows you the opportunity to know God better. It's easy to stay on the interstate. It requires no effort whatsoever. The interstate allows you to go with the flow. If you are like me, you are ready to take the next exit off. Life starts at the off ramp. There is a different road out there—the road less traveled. It offers excitement and adventure. I'm sure if you want to find God, he is more likely to be there on the old road than he is on the interstate. Trust me. It's worth the time and the effort to find him out there on the old highway.

Finding the Old Road

I'm sure that we are all on some type of journey in our lives. My journey is to rediscover God and to determine where he is at work and how I can join him in that effort. In order to do that, you have to travel down the old road because that's where you can find God. God is showing me that the old road is a metaphor and a guide for us on how we should live our lives for Christ. But first you have to find where the old road is.

For years I have traveled the back roads across America, especially Route 66. The old road is anything but easy to find. Over 90% of Route 66 still exists, but you won't find it on any road map. If you do find it, it's often difficult to follow because you really never know if you're on Route 66 or some other old pavement. You can purchase special maps, but it's no guarantee that you will be able to follow it accurately. Route 66 now has many names. Depending on which state you are in, it could be a county, state or local route designation.

Route 66 was commissioned in 1926 and continued to be a work-in-progress for the next 50 years. It went through multiple pavements, bypasses, and upgrades throughout its history. What makes it especially difficult to follow Route 66 are many abandoned sections and multiple routes. With so many different alignments, it requires the driver to be dedicated and passionate in his or her efforts to adequately follow the road. Our life as a Christian also requires the same effort if we are to stay on course.

So how do we find the old road? First, we have to believe in our heart that God is real, that he sent his son to die for our sins and that he rose again from the grave. When we do this and accept Jesus as our personal Savior, we are saved. That is the basic requirement for entry to the old road. This is when our journey begins. As incredible as this sounds, for many Christians this is as far as they will go. In fact, instead of journeying down the old road, they would rather detour back to the interstate.

For those of us who wish to journey farther, it requires us to develop a personal relationship with our Savior. We need to know who God is. What does he want? What is his character, his nature and his value system? We can travel the old road by learning his Word and then putting it into practice. We can also observe our fellow Christians and learn from their experiences. And through prayer we can begin the process of understanding how God works in our lives.

As we journey down the old highway, we will encounter the next road sign. As we begin to know God personally, we will be faced with a decision that each Christian must face. Will we make him Lord of our lives? And how much are we willing to turn over to him? Whether we realize it or not, each of us will start to negotiate with God. We are ready to make a deal. We tell God, if you give me what I want, I will turn this percentage of my life over to you. All I can say, after many years of experience, is good luck with that one.

143

God is not in the business of making deals or negotiating. With him it's all or nothing. But as we travel down the old highway, we will continue to try to offer God a deal.

What we really want is to follow both the old highway and the interstate. That way we can have the best of both worlds. I'm convinced that many Christians are miserable because they try to travel both roads. At some point along the journey, you are going to learn that it's one road or the other. As we continue on, some of us will start turning over more of our lives to God, and we will reach a tipping point where we start to ask the question about what his will is for us and how we can experience his presence in our lives. Can we hear his voice? Absolutely! If we are prepared to stay on the old road.

We stay on the old road by diving into the Word of God. As a result, God will reveal himself more clearly through circumstances and prayer. God can speak to us in any way he desires. I have never failed to experience God fully in nature. I have some of my most significant encounters climbing mountains and exploring canyons. It will be different for every person. There is no formula you can follow. Remember, the old road has many curves, dips and corners, and they are different on every old highway.

As you experience God more fully, you will encounter the next mile post on your journey. The only way to fully know God is to recognize that he is Spirit. We will have to go beyond our logic and reasoning and realize that if we are to journey further along the old road, we will need to embrace the supernatural. These are the things that we cannot see. We must allow the Holy Spirit to lead and be in charge of our lives. No matter what choices we make in life, there are only three ways we can approach any decision we make. We can either do it God's way, our way, or the world's way. Each way is unique from the others and operates by different laws and principles. If you are to operate under the supernatural and continue on the old road, you will be required to embrace God's way of doing things. Logic and reason can only take you so far. But the supernatural will bring you into the presence of God.

As you look for God out on the old road and hear his voice, you will reach the final mile post. This milepost will be the key to knowing how God is at work in the world and to knowing how to join him. Some people call it a crisis of faith. The very thing you want the most or that part of your life that you're holding on to, God will place himself in front of as a barrier. You will have to make a decision. Are you prepared to finally make him Lord of your life? I'm convinced the reason many of us don't see God at work in the world is because we have failed the crisis of faith. This is the part of our journey on the old highway where we stop negotiating with God. Remember, we're not buying a car here. God does not negotiate. He offers his deal and his plan. It's a "take it or leave it" proposition. When we stop negotiating with God, we start living by faith in what God wants for us.

After you pass this final milepost, you will start seeing God at work in places you never imagined. The interstate will be a past memory, and you will wonder why you ever spent so much time there. Traveling the old road is about building the Kingdom of God. And the Kingdom that God is building will look vastly different than anything we can imagine. Are you ready to take the off ramp? God is out there on the old road looking for you.

15   The Matrix

Congratulations! You have made it to the end of the book. If you've made it this far, then you are a true believer. There's no question that you want to think for yourself. Like so many of us, you do not want to be defined by today's media culture. You want to know the truth, and you see things in a different light. It would be convenient to go along with predictable patterns and accept what the media culture is telling us to believe about our world and about ourselves. But you have decided to go a different way. But what now?

I'm sure that before you read this book you were unhappy with the direction of our culture. You are as frustrated as I am. You're wondering why Christianity is not changing the world. Christ gave us the Great Commission to go tell the world about his love and his forgiveness. But it seems that no one cares anymore. In some ways, it seems like Christianity has lost its enthusiasm. What are we living for? If not for Christ, then what?

This book asks the question "Is the media culture a crisis or an opportunity? I believe it is both. But just like you, as I wrote this book, it was an eye-opener for me as well. God revealed to me that the media culture does not have to be a crisis if we embrace the opportunities and join him at work.

The best place to start is to embrace the Five Principles contained in this book. If we are going to change our world and build the Kingdom of God, it will start with you. If you earnestly seek God through prayer, he will give you the answers necessary to bring about a change in the direction of our culture.

Writing this final chapter was a struggle. Which direction should I go? My original version was a bit too preachy. Like you, I am beyond that point. I would only be preaching to the choir. You know there's a problem with the media culture. You see beyond the common trappings of sexuality, language, violence and nudity. You understand the media culture's core message is changing the face of Christianity.

So I asked God how to finish this book. First, if we are going to build the Kingdom of God, we are going to have to change the media culture. But we cannot change the media culture until more of our brothers and sisters in the Body of Christ are aware of the strategies, influence and control that the media culture is exerting over our daily lives. It's like we are asleep.

As I said earlier in my introduction, I run every day. And while I was out on one of my runs, God said that those who read this book need to go and watch the movie, *The Matrix*. Why *The Matrix*? Because *The Matrix* is an allegory for the state of Christianity today. If you haven't seen the movie, I will give you the basic rundown.

The matrix is a simulated reality or computer program that was created to enslave mankind. People go about their daily lives unaware that they are actually asleep in suspended animation. Everything they see before them is a lie. In actuality, humans live in a pod connected to wires and are used to generate energy for a machine-based society. I know this is a lot of science fiction. But the truth is the concept of the matrix is very real because, in some ways, we are living it today.

In the movie, our main hero, Neo, is given a choice. He can go back to the matrix and continue to live his life and be happy, or he can learn the truth about his existence. He is offered a red pill that will reveal the truth and a blue pill that will take him back to the matrix. We are all given that same choice today. Our red pill is the Bible. If we want to understand the truth, we will read it and believe it.

The matrix was created to keep mankind happy and content. But mankind is living in a perceived reality. They can feel. They can see. They can hear. They can smell. They can touch. The world they believe in exists only in a computer program. The media culture has led to the creation of our own self-made matrix, which has striking similarities to the one in the film. We want a matrix that is safe, comfortable, convenient and happy. But is this the kind of life God talks about in the Bible? The media culture would have us believe that life revolves around our wants and that we are the center of our own personal universe.

In 2 Corinthians 6:5-7 Paul writes about his suffering. "We have been beaten, put in jail, faced angry mobs, worked to exhaustion, endured sleepless nights and gone without food. We have proved ourselves by our purity, our understanding, our patience, our kindness, our sincere love, and the power of the Holy Spirit. We have faithfully preached the truth." *(NLT)* Paul's experiences may be a bit extreme by today's standards, but proclaiming the Gospel and standing up for the truth always comes with a price. The Word of God makes that very clear.

James 1:3 says "For when your faith is tested, your endurance has a chance to grow. So let it grow, for when your endurance is fully developed, you will be strong in character and ready for anything." *(NLT)* We will not grow in our faith without tests. It is fair to say that the life we live now is not about our comfort but is more like running a race. If we want to finish the race strong, we must train so that our endurance will strengthen over time.

2 Corinthians 4:18 says "So we don't look at the troubles we can see right now, rather, we look forward to what we have not yet seen. For the troubles we see will soon be over, but the joys to come will last forever." *(NLT)* And Jesus said in John 16:33 "I have told you all this so that you may have peace in me. Here on earth you will have many trials and sorrows but take heart because I have overcome the world." *(NLT)* This is not the message we would like to hear, but it is the truth. By insulating ourselves, we are living a lie. The media culture has created a matrix that is not real. Our purpose is to serve the will of God. Jesus said that you must give up your life for him. We are told that this life will have its troubles, trials and sorrows. But beyond our self-made matrix exists a life we have not seen that will bring us joys that last for an eternity.

We live in a physical world that looks and feels authentic. It, like the matrix, is only a perceived reality. Most of us live life as if the world we live in is the only one that will ever exist. We are interested in building an earthly kingdom instead of the Kingdom of God. But the Kingdom of God is the real world. Somehow we have forgotten this.

Revelation 21:1 says "Then I saw a new heaven and a new earth for the old heaven and the old earth had disappeared. And the sea was also gone. And I saw the Holy City, the new Jerusalem, coming down from God out of heaven like a beautiful bride prepared for her husband. I heard a loud shout from the throne, 'Look, the home of God is now among his people. He will live with them and they will be his people. God himself will be with them. He will remove all of their sorrows, and there will be no more death or sorrow or crying or pain, for the old world and its evils are gone forever'". *(NLT)* As Christians, this is our future, our promise, our destiny and our hope. The matrix that we have created can offer none of this.

2 Corinthians 5:1 says "For we know that when this earthly tent we live in is taken down (that is, when we die and leave this earthly body) we will have a house in heaven, an eternal body made for us by God himself and not by human hands. We grow weary in our present bodies, and we long for the day when we put on our heavenly bodies like new clothing." *(NLT)* The matrix has confused us concerning which existence is real. Just like those in the movie, they had no idea they were living in a false reality. We will have a new body and a new home in heaven that is eternal. The world we live in today will no longer exist. Even if you are an atheist or agnostic, science tells us that one day the sun will explode. There will be no evidence that the human race ever existed in the universe, at least not in the physical place called earth.

Our own bodies are a matrix. They do not reflect who we really are. We are more than flesh and bone. We are spirit made in the image of God. Do not believe what you see in the mirror or what the media culture tells us about ourselves is who you are. We are more than that.

Everything you are working for, whether it be wealth, power, or influence, will not exist. What we pass on to our children, grandchildren and great-grandchildren will not last forever. So why are we living in this matrix and pretending that it is real? Why are we putting so much energy, effort and work into building an earthly kingdom? The only real existence is the one that God is preparing for us. If you grasp this concept and really think about it, it will change how you approach life.

How do you and I convince our fellow brothers and sisters in Christ to give up their safe and comfortable matrix? God already knows what you need. Matthew 6:25 says "That is why I tell you not to worry about everyday life—whether you have enough food and drink, or enough clothes to wear. Isn't life more than food, and your body more than clothing?" Verses 32-34 say, "These things dominate the thoughts of unbelievers, but your heavenly Father already knows all your needs. Seek the Kingdom of God above all else, and live righteously, and he will give you everything you need. So don't worry about tomorrow, for tomorrow will bring its own worries. Today's trouble is enough for today." *(NLT)*

We have come to the heart of the issue. The Kingdom of God must be first in our lives. But you already know that. I wrote about the matrix, not to convince you that the media culture is making it easy for us to live for ourselves but because God wants us to see that this is the state of Christianity today. We are trapped by our own self-made matrix. God wants to set us free. We have a choice: Serve God or make the matrix our master.

You and I are like the character Morfius in the film. He is the one who offers the red pill to Neo. By taking the red pill, the truth about the matrix would be revealed. We have to do the same thing, one person at a time. If you believe the principles I share with you in this book, then you have a part to play.

When I started writing this book, I was convinced that raising up media missionaries to Hollywood was the answer to changing the media culture. But God showed me this is only part of the answer. You are the other part because you are a media missionary to your friends, family and local church. Because you have read this book, the change has already begun. You are the answer to solving the media culture crisis. I titled this book *The Red Pill, The Cure for Today's Mass Media Culture*. You are part of that cure. Without you at the local church level, nothing will change. Yes, it may be possible to send a few media missionaries to Hollywood, or a few more people may pray for Christians and non-Christians working in the industry. *But that will result in no significant change without your participation at the local level. You can be the one to offer people the red pill. The best place to start is to get others to read this book.*

No amount of preaching or lecturing will convince people to take the red pill. Only the Holy Spirit can reveal the truth. Allow God to use you. Pray for those around you that their eyes will be opened to the truth about the media culture crisis. Use the example of the matrix for your inspiration. I believe God gave us this revelation to help us understand the spiritual forces that are working against us.

Consider the following suggestions. Go back to Chapter 11 and read the Hero's Journey to see how God can use you to be a media missionary wherever you are planted. The plan starts in Chapter 12 with what you can do in the first seven days and all the way through the first five years. These are practical suggestions that are the nuts and bolts for changing our culture. Do not let them overwhelm you. Look for a place to begin. Starting a film night or prayer group within your circle of family and friends is a big deal. It's a perfect way to offer people the red pill without having to lecture them. Celebrate small victories. Trust me. I have tried preaching and lecturing over the years about the media culture. It doesn't work.

Look for natural allies. I'm sure there are others around you who are concerned about building the Kingdom of God. Ask God to lead those people to you. Look for media, such as movies and television, that does not support the basic teachings of today's media culture. As I have written, that type of media does exist. There are those who are not embracing a lifestyle that makes consumerism, materialism, wealth and power the center of everything in life worth achieving. They need our support and encouragement. Remember these are the things that lead us to the matrix. When we put our wants first, we have embraced the message of the media culture.

And seek out organizations that can help you as well as support you in your growth as a media missionary. I have already written about the Hollywood Prayer Network and hollywoodconnect.com. They are good places to find resources to help you.

The best advice I can offer is to recognize where God is at work. I know He is already working in media and entertainment. He is also working in the lives of those who make media in Hollywood and elsewhere. He is undoubtedly at work around you. The single biggest mistake that most Christians make is that we fail to see God at work. As a media missionary, it is critical that you see where God is working and join him in that effort.

It is impossible to do anything through our own strength and abilities. When we think we've got it covered or that we don't need God's help, it will end in spiritual failure. John 15:5 makes it clear that without Jesus we can accomplish nothing. Our efforts may appear to be successful in terms of how the world evaluates success but certainly not in terms of how God evaluates success. Either God is at work in the world, or he is not. I'm convinced that God seeks a partnership. It's when we join him in his work that things happen.

For too many Christians, God has become more of a concept than a reality. In order for God to be a reality, we have to know him and experience his character and nature. We come to know him by reading his Word daily, spending personal time alone in prayer, and listening to his voice. As he reveals himself to you, you can see him more clearly. We need God, who is real, not a god who is a concept. God has called us to be a part of the solution to use the media culture crisis for an opportunity to reveal God's truth and glory.

The most significant thing you can do as a media missionary is to pray. Pray for wisdom on how we can change today's media culture. Pray for Hollywood and the entertainment industry. Pray that Christians working in the media will have favor and opportunities to make media that reflects God's truth and glory. Pray for non-Christians that they will receive Christ. Also, I encourage you to pray that God will raise up media missionaries to Hollywood and the entertainment industry. You have the red pill and you know the truth. Pray that God will give you opportunities to know when and how to offer the red pill to those God will put in your pathway.

If you believe that God is calling you to Hollywood or the entertainment industry, I encourage you to not allow anything or anybody to discourage you. We need your passion and your desire to reach Hollywood and beyond. God will give you the answers you need to fulfill your calling as a media missionary. In this case, one size does not fit everyone. God has an individual plan for you. Your task is to discover that. No one can give you a roadmap or a blueprint on how to be a media missionary. Only the Holy Spirit can provide that. Please don't settle for second best. I encourage you to make media that is excellent, truthful and honest.

The road into Hollywood and the entertainment industry is difficult and challenging. Your relationship with God is essential. If you are going to change the entertainment industry, you must be changed from within and allow the Holy Spirit to control your thoughts, actions and motives. Don't allow the industry to change you into something that is unpleasing to God.

I have talked to people who have gone to Hollywood and have forgotten the most important thing: continue to seek a deep and committed relationship with Christ. Find a support system, a church, or a fellowship group that will surround you with prayer and support. Do not go it alone.

For us who are media missionaries in our local church body, we must provide you the support, prayers and encouragement that you need as a media missionary working in Hollywood and the entertainment industry.

If we work together, we can dismantle the matrix that many have come to accept as reality. Let's help them realize it is a lie and that they have been deceived. This is our end game to spread the Truth and offer the red pill to all those who need to hear this message.

God has burned this message on my heart and mind, and I can't let go of it. Or maybe I should say it won't let go of me. Just when we think it's over, God has a plan. And he wants us to be play a part. Listen to the call to a "brave new frontier" where we have not gone before. God is opening the door. What is in your hand? Can you pray? Can you teach? Can you give? Can you write? What is your story? Consider your part. Use your influence. Engage your talents. Utilize your resources.

God is cheering us on. Remember in Deuteronomy 31:6 what God said to Joshua. "So be strong and courageous! Do not be afraid and do not panic before them. For the Lord your God will personally go ahead of you. He will neither fail or abandon you." *NLT*

Appendix 1   The Perfect Storm

Wikipedia's encyclopedia says that a perfect storm is an expression that describes an event where a rare combination of circumstances will aggravate a situation drastically.

When a series of events came together at the right time and place in our nation's history, we created a perfect storm, which caused media to be transformed into a force capable of creating a media culture. What rare combination of circumstances has made the media a significant and powerful force in our culture? When did television, movies and other forms of media stop being entertainment and become a media culture capable of shaping our beliefs, attitudes and behaviors?

The modern media culture developed over four distinct time periods starting with the development of the film industry in the early part of the 20th Century continuing to the creation of the digital age in the late 1990s. The story behind the perfect storm is also interwoven with the so-called mythical American Dream. To understand the perfect storm and how we are influenced by today's media, we must understand how the American Dream has been manipulated. *The U.S. Attitudes on the American Dream*, a recent survey by the Xavier University Institute for Politics, states that 60% of Americans believe it will be more difficult for them to achieve the American Dream than for their parents. Sixty-eight percent of Americans say it will be even more difficult for their children to achieve the American Dream.

So what is the American Dream and how is it tied to the media culture? More importantly, how has it changed the face of Christianity over the past few years? According to this survey, most white, middle class Americans see the American Dream in terms of financial security. African Americans tend to see it as wealth. Only 8% of those surveyed viewed it as a sense of happiness. Mike Ford, founding director of Xavier University Institute, says the American Dream "is a time-honored core belief that we have for ourselves as Americans—that the next generation will have it better than we did." If Ford is right, that means the American Dream is always a moving target. It will continue to grow and expand.

"Having it better" is a subjective concept. Who is going to define what that means? I'm convinced that powerful interests which "control the media" have used the American Dream to their advantage by creating a culture where materialism and consumerism have become the primary force in our lives. "Having it better" for some means a bigger house, more cars, a better school, and more money than the previous generation. We believe that we fail to achieve the American Dream if we don't achieve these goals. But how can the American Dream continue to expand for each future generation if it continues to be based on the accumulation of material things? Is there a limit to how much we can own? At what point is enough, enough?

Have we turned the American Dream from opportunity and freedom to our ability to use and maximize our credit cards? Can we spend our way to the American Dream as individuals or as a nation? The media culture must convince us that having it all *is* the American Dream and without it we cannot be happy.

Is achieving the American Dream and building the Kingdom of God the same goal? Or are they different? Some would suggest that Christianity reflects a value system that is more consistent with media culture values than Biblical values. If achieving the American Dream as defined by today's media culture has become the new primary goal for Christians, it would certainly suggest that serving God and placing him first in our lives is no longer our primary goal. If all of this is true, it helps to explain why Christianity has lost its influence within our society. Shouldn't faith be the primary influence on culture rather than the media?

In 2004 George Barna conducted a study titled *Faith and People's Behaviors*. He used 19 core lifestyle choices as the basis of his study. He concluded that faith had only a minor affect on people's behaviors. He found very little difference in how Christians, atheists, or agnostics applied the 19 lifestyle choices in their daily lives. It would appear that whether you call yourself a Christian or not, we all now seem to have developed a blended worldview. What we all have in common is an interest to pursue a lifestyle based on consumerism. We are becoming defined by what we own.

The perfect storm has created a world where media and culture are now indistinguishable from each other. To understand where the media culture will take us in the future requires an understanding of how it all came together.

The First Media Age

Let's start with an understanding of the four modern media ages. The First Media Age or The Golden Age of Hollywood started at the beginning of the 20th Century. It was the beginning of mass communication and entertainment as we know it today. New technologies such as radio and film ushered in the age of modernism and served as a melting pot of ideas and philosophies.

Much of America had changed since the beginning of the Industrial Revolution. Most people lived on farms in rural areas isolated from outside influences. As a result, family and the immediate community had the biggest impact on world views, religious beliefs, values and morals. Before The Golden Age of Hollywood, most people rarely traveled more than 20 miles from their homes. All of that changed in the latter part of the 19th Century as people moved from the countryside into cities due to the availability of jobs.

There were new influences to be found around every corner. The First Media Age with its emphasis on technology proved to be one of those influences. Modernism was one of the most significant philosophies that prevailed in the First Media Age. Modernism offered a changing society and a new future. It championed that science and reason could explain the mysteries of the universe, the origins of life itself. We were told that science and reason could unlock the answers to life's questions.

During this time, people were fascinated and infatuated with anything modern. They had a desire for knowledge, understanding and enlightenment. Modernism provided a framework that helped to explain life's mysteries. Radio and film developed during this period and offered a conduit where these ideas could be shared. There were also plenty of subtle philosophies floating around that found a home in the new, emerging media age such as Marxism, Darwinism and evolution.

Radio offered people an opportunity to hear information and news as it happened and also provided the first home entertainment experience where the family could gather around an electronic media device. It caused the world to become smaller, practically overnight.

Perhaps the most influential institution in the First Media Age was the creation and development of the motion picture industry which today we call Hollywood. The industry was established by Jewish immigrants from Eastern Europe. Looking for new opportunities, they established the first film industry on the East Coast. The industry got its start in 1891 when Thomas Edison applied for a patent on his new camera called the kinetoscope. Jewish immigrants embraced this new industry by opening Nickelodeons, nickel theaters dedicated solely to film exhibition.

Thomas Edison was determined to dominate the industry by controlling production, distribution and exhibition of films. Because of a combination of legal pressures, threats and coercion, most of the European Jewish immigrants fled west to California and decided to produce their own movies. The American Dream was well entrenched in these early pioneers of the film industry. Carl Laemmle formed The Independent Motion Picture Company, which became Universal Studios. Adolph Zukor formed Famous Players and Famous Plays, which later became Paramount. William Fox formed what would become known as 20th Century Fox. Louis B. Meyer would become the president of one of the most powerful studios in Hollywood's history, MGM, the so-called Dream Factory. In 1915, the independent Jewish producers were victorious in court when Edison's efforts to control the entire motion picture industry was ruled as an illegal trust.

By the early 1920s, men like Carl Laemmle, William Fox, and Louis B. Meyer came to control and dominate Hollywood and movie making for decades to come. Amazingly, a few individuals would now have the power and influence to create movies for the entire American population and the world. They would decide which films would be made and which ones would not, which ideas would be expressed and which ones would be discarded. They would decide what was important and what was not. Never had so much power been placed in the hands of so few men.

In the 1930s, Louis B. Meyer, President of MGM, viewed America as a glittering new frontier, decent but tough-minded, full of God-fearing but gun-slinging Americans who were shrewd, unpredictable and unbeatable but also open-hearted and family loving. And he depicted this view in the movies he produced.

Meyer and his fellow movie moguls offered a vision of America that people wanted to believe and were willing to accept. It made us feel good about ourselves. Meyer understood that it was good for business. The majority of studio heads had no political or social agenda. They were interested in one thing and one thing only—making money. Was their view of American life realistic? It offered no racism, prejudice or social injustice. It defined America as a land of opportunity, champion of individuals, and defender of the poor. It offered no insight into how Americans really lived their daily lives.

The moviegoer saw no instances of alcoholism or domestic abuse in family lives. In Meyer's world, good always triumphed, and evil was punished. Every family embraced moral values and practiced faith and patriotism. The cowboys were good, and the Indians were bad. This view of America has perpetuated itself to this very day. We think of the 1930s through the 1950s as the "good old days". In some ways, Hollywood had no choice but to reflect these views because that's what Americans wanted to believe. This was reinforced by a production code, which was imposed on filmmakers by both Protestant and Catholic churches.

We came to view ourselves by what we saw in the movies in the 1930s and 1940s and television programs from the 1950s, including shows such as *Leave it to Beaver* and *Father Knows Best*, as a representation of the real America. But in reality it is a mythology created by Meyer and his fellow studio heads that created a version of America that only existed in the movies. This is evidence of the power of media—that we are willing to accept a lie over the truth because the lie makes us feel better about ourselves. It raises the question of what else are we willing to accept as the truth.

Because of Meyer's efforts, Americans fell in love with entertainment. By the 1930s, most Americans went to the movies at least twice weekly. It cut across every demographic and social class. And this occurred during the worst depression that the United States has ever experienced. Americans had a desire for escapism. Movies were hot.

America had developed a love affair with Hollywood and celebrity.

And to take it a step further, Meyer and other movie moguls sold Americans *their* version of the mythical American Dream. America was founded on ideas such as fair play, equality, freedom, justice and the pursuit of happiness. The movie moguls took this idea of the pursuit of happiness and turned it into the pursuit of materialism and wealth. The American Dream became less about idealism and more about commercialism. The American founders' idea of the American dream got hijacked by Hollywood, and they used the myth of the American Dream for their own benefit. Hollywood was willing to sell people what they wanted them to believe instead of the truth.

The 1930s was a time when many Americans stood in bread lines. America was in the middle of a great depression. One-third of the work force was unemployed. The great dust bowls in the Midwest were in the process of turning America into a wasteland. But Hollywood was offering up glamour and a lifestyle that seemed to be from a different world, one that was out of reach for the average American. It was a version of the American Dream based on wealth and materialism. The ideas that fueled the American Dream are complex. These ideas were powerful and capable of shaping the destiny of our nation, including our spiritual direction.

In the years to come, the battle will rage on. What is the American Dream? Who will define it and for what purpose?

The First Media Age laid the foundation on which all future media ages would be built. Worldviews and various philosophies may have been subtle by today's standards but, nevertheless, the seeds had been sown.

The Second Media Age

The Second Media Age or the Age of Television started in the late 1940s with the dawn of television and clearly had the greatest, single impact on our culture than any other technological development in the 20th Century. Its development helped to create today's modern media culture. At the beginning of 1950, few Americans owned a television set. They were relatively expensive, and the prices would not significantly drop for at least a decade. But by 1954, 56% of Americans had a television set, and by 1962 that number reached 90%. Why did television grow so rapidly? It came along at the right time and found the perfect companion in the form of consumerism in the 1950s.

Just like a dam, the development of television and consumerism had been delayed for years thanks to a worldwide depression and World War II. By the late 1940s, Americans had put there lives on hold (in some cases for two decades). They had delayed marriage, starting a family and, in most cases, just living life. There was a pent-up desire to live life to its fullest. There was perhaps a sense of entitlement, which is easy to understand considering what America had just gone through—depression, war, death and destruction.

Many people reasoned "if I survived all this, there must be a reason, perhaps a better life for myself and my family". They wanted to believe in the American Dream. But what is the American Dream? Is it based on freedom, justice and the pursuit of happiness? Or did the new emerging media have a different view of the American Dream and was more than willing to sell it to us. It now had the perfect delivery system, television.

How did all of these pieces come together? During wartime, American factories worked around the clock at maximum production to produce tanks, airplanes, ammunition, and all other forms of wartime materials. Nothing like this had ever happened before. The industrial might of the United States was unstoppable and was the clear and determining factor in victory over the Axis powers. But all of that stopped in August 1945.

The American Version of Consumerism

What would happen to all of those workers and factories? How do you retool for peacetime, continue to grow the American economy, and provide the goods and services to fuel the pursuit of the American Dream. The American version of consumerism began right at the dawn of television. But this wasn't ordinary consumerism. The world had never seen anything like it. It was mass consumerism at an unprecedented level. Factories soon produced automobiles, refrigerators, stoves, furniture, building materials for new homes, washers, dryers, television sets, etc.

The consumerism that developed during this period was based on three principles. First, products were designed to be obsolete or fail within a certain amount of time, which required the consumer to buy the product several times over. Second, each year a new model would be introduced with new features and benefits. This advertising concept would become known as the *new and improved model*, but in reality it was the same product with a few modifications. A marketing strategy was developed to convince us that without the new and improved model or product we were out of touch or incomplete. The third principle was to convince the public to upgrade to the next model or to purchase the next new product. The idea was to keep the consumer unhappy and believing that the next purchase would finally be the purchase that would make us feel complete. But the fact is, no matter how many things we purchase, we will never reach that level of happiness.

Marketing and advertising were designed to keep us reaching for something that was always out-of-reach. We all became good consumers. In the early 1950s, the commercial application of television started in earnest. Television networks were formed, such as ABC, NBC, and CBS, and offered different types of programming from variety/talk shows, sitcoms, drama and news programs.

Commercialization of Television

So who would pay for the development of programming? The answer was advertisers within the programming itself as well as paid ads. Commercial television led to the beginning of the modern development of media. It created a relationship between business, media and culture. It is based on a triangular relationship with business and media at the bottom of the pyramid and culture at the top of the pyramid. Business needed a demand to fuel consumerism. Media, such as television, needed financial resources to develop programming. The two formed a relationship which served each other's interests.

Television had the ability to influence culture (shared beliefs and behavior patterns or general consciousness), particularly how we spend our money.

Advertisers used this to create the desire for goods and services. Americans came to believe that what they saw on television through advertising and entertainment programs was a lifestyle that they believed was achievable. This was a version of the American Dream presented by Wall Street and the entertainment industry. Television and consumerism were the perfect companions. Television shows like *Father Knows Best*, *Leave It to Beaver*, *Make Room for Daddy*, and *Ozzie and Harriet* depicted a nice home in the suburbs with a white picket fence and a back yard, a car in the driveway, new and shiny appliances and a lifestyle of comfort and convenience. You can only imagine, after watching this night after night, the type of impact it would have on our collective consciousness as a society. Television would help to commercialize the way we viewed life.

This desire for what we saw ultimately became a demand for products and services. Television was capable of creating an emotional response. It impacted our actions, and we started buying the products and services offered. We were convinced we could not live without them. And what about those who felt locked out of the American Dream? African-Americans and other minorities wanted the same things but were not permitted access into the mainstream economic forces emerging in the 1950s. They would feel resentment toward a society that talked about the American Dream but was unwilling to make it possible for them. Minorities would demand equal access to the American Dream in the years ahead thanks, in part, to how they viewed the American Dream on television.

To summarize, the formula for consumerism is Influence + Desire = Demand. To be fair, we understand that advertising is a form of manipulation. But what I think we fail to understand is that all programming, entertainment and news has become a form of manipulation that has fueled our quest for consumerism (which is based on somebody else's idea of the American Dream).

Consumerism is only part of the puzzle. The 1950s was the pivotal point in history wherein today's modern media culture emerged. Marshall McLuhan proposes in his book, *Understanding Media, the Extensions of Man*, a theory that the medium is an extension of our ideas, senses and thought processes. In this case, the medium he is talking about is the development of television. He states, "This extension will always bring about some form of change within culture. This change is often unnoticed. We tend to focus on the content of the message but overlook the character of the medium or the process of change, which ultimately occurs." In McLuhan's theory, television becomes the message.

This theory was not well understood at the time of the book in 1964, and many still have failed to understand its implications. Simply put, it doesn't matter what's on television or at the movies. It's not about the content. In the 1950s, we had the most family-friendly, G-rated, positive programming that has ever been produced. When television became a reality throughout America, did we really look close enough to see how it was changing us? Overnight, the television set became the most important piece of furniture in the household. It was given a prime spot in the living room. Every night, the American family gathered around the television set for three or four hours. This occurred virtually everywhere. Nothing like it had ever happened before.

The Ed Sullivan Show became "must see" television. The fact is everything became "must see" television. Did we really care what was on? We were fascinated with the images. The technology changed our behavior patterns. We stopped communicating, playing games or just pitching the ball in the back yard. It was during this time that the term "TV dinners" was coined. We would now bring the TV in during the dinner hour. The television became the center of attention instead of discussing what was occurring in our daily lives.

To this very day, do we really understand the impact this new technology had on our culture? We now just accept these things as natural. But, believe it or not, there was a time before television.

When you combine the forces of consumerism with the new medium of television, they help break down established behavior patterns. American society started to change. We were more captivated by what was on television than what was going on in real life.

How does this fit in with all the social problems that have dramatically increased in American society since the 1950s? Teen pregnancy, suicide, drug and alcohol abuse, the breakdown of the family, decline in morals and values, and divorce are some of the problems we are all aware of.

Could it be that the American family is the ultimate casualty thanks to the technological development of television and the rise of a new form of consumerism? I certainly think there is a case to be made. What price are we willing to pay for this new version of the American Dream? A house in the suburbs? A new car? A pool? A boat? And that is only the beginning. A 2,000 square foot home, or is it a 4,000 square foot home, or what about a 6,000 square foot home?

When is enough, enough? In fact enough is never enough. We changed our attitudes toward everything. We worked longer hours. Working weekends wasn't just an option, it became the rule. Fifty- to seventy-hour weeks became the standard. And it was easy to justify. We were doing it for our family so they could have a better life. But did this stuff really bring happiness?

But that wasn't even enough. It became apparent that soon both parents would have to work to continue this pursuit of consumerism. What effect did it have on our families? The television set became the new babysitter. All across America we were in the process of creating a new generation that was raised on television. Parents were too busy and worked too many hours because they believed they were doing the right thing. But, in the process, it was our children who were being neglected.

Could this explain why so many social problems dramatically increased in the 1960s and years to come? Television helped condition an entire generation of baby boomers born between 1946 and 1964 to accept a reality based on the images that were presented in the medium of television. They were the first generation to be primarily influenced and motivated by the power of image-based media. The TV generation would become the powerbrokers and ultimately would lead a new revolution to reinvent television during the development of cable and satellite technology.

By the 1970s, media and culture had combined to create a media culture. For years, many had argued that media was a reflection of culture. In other words, the sex and violence that was on television and at the movies merely reflected what was happening in society. Others argued that media drove and created culture. But by the end of the Second Media Age it really didn't matter.

Maybe the best way I can illustrate my argument is a speech from Edward R. Murrow, one of the nation's first pioneers in television journalism. In fact, he wrote the book. The speech was given in 1958 in Chicago before television and radio executives. Historians have called it the wires and lights speech. His words are chilling and prophetic and they should cause all of us to seriously think about the state of our own existence. "This just might do nobody any good. At the end of this discourse, a few people may accuse this reporter of filling his own comfortable nest, and your organization may be accused of having given hospitality to heretical and even dangerous thoughts, but the elaborate structure of networks, advertising agencies, and sponsors will not be shaken or altered. It is my desire, if not my duty, to try to talk to you journeymen with some candor about what is happening to radio and television. Our history will be what we make it. And if there are any historians about fifty or a hundred years from now, and there should be preserved the kinescopes for one week of all three networks, they will there find recorded in black in white, or color, evidence of decadence, escapism and insulation from the realities of the world in which we live.

We are currently wealthy, fat, comfortable and compliant. We have currently a built-in allergy to unpleasant and disturbing information. Our mass media reflects this. But unless we get up off our fat surpluses and recognize that television in the main is being used to distract, delude, amuse, and insulate us, then television and those who finance it, those who look at it and those who work at it, may see a totally different picture too late."

You have to remember that Murrow said this over 50 years ago. I'm sure he would be absolutely amazed if he could see the extent of today's mass media and the rise of our media culture. Edward R. Murrow saw the future. He realized the power of television and its influence throughout on society. Murrow raised several intriguing questions. Are we being distracted from the truth. Are we insulated from the realities of the world we live in? Has it been done by design? Let's put it this way. Is the media culture a form of a new drug? I'm convinced we're being medicated into compliance. For the most part, we really don't understand what's happening around us. We are told what to think in a nice way that suggests that we are making our own decisions. But are we?

By the 1970s, media and culture had combined to create a media culture. For years, many had argued that media was a reflection of culture. In other words, the sex and violence that was on television and at the movies merely reflected what was happening in society. Others argued that media drove and created culture. But by the end of the Second Media Age it really didn't matter.

During the 1960s and 1970s, America had gone through many upheavals, including an unpopular war in Vietnam, racial discrimination, riots, and scandals such as Watergate. This created a general mistrust of our institutions, such as government and religion. Many young people felt misled and lied to. There was a sense of anger and frustration.

Many church leaders argue that the cultural revolution and counterculture of the 1960s has lead to a decline of morals and values within our society. They believe that most of the social issues that we face today is a direct result of the cultural revolution.

I grew up in the 1960s. It seemed to me that by 1968 the world was coming unglued. America's major cities were in flames. There were riots, open conflict on the streets, and an unpopular war that no one understood. There was a sense of fear and anxiety. Could we survive this? Looking back, my question is how much impact did the second media age have on shaping these events.

As I have stated, the parents of baby boomers in the late 1940s and 1950s embraced a new form of consumerism which led to a new level of materialism not seen before in America. I argue that it was influenced and controlled by the new emerging media culture fed by the new technology of television. Instead of addressing issues such as racism and poverty, America entered into an age that embraced a self-serving attitude. Baby boomers by the 1960s were looking for meaning and purpose, especially the children of privilege. There had to be something more to life than just material things. They found hope in the new young president, John F. Kennedy, who talked about service and a call to action to serve mankind.

Two events clearly opened the door to the coming social revolution. What most people failed to take into account was the major role television and the media culture played in shaping these events. The first was the loss of hope when John F. Kennedy was assasinated. His presidency played out on television from the start to the very end. Those events viewed on television had an enormous influence on the psyche of America's young people. Somehow, at the age of seven, I realized without fully understanding it that America would never be the same again. The images of John F. Kennedy's entire presidency that were played out on television were crystallized in my mind. And I suspect in the minds of my generation as well.

The second catalyst was the Vietnam war which, once again, was played out each night in the living rooms of America. Several historians have argued that if television had been available in the 1940s America may not have had the determination or the stomach to endure World War II. My contention is that these two events opened the door to the social revolution of the 1960s, and the media culture provided a framework that made it possible.

The Third Media Age/MTV

As the Third Media Age or the Cable Age approached, philosophies such as secular humanism and cosmic (new age) humanism found a home in this atmosphere. This age had a clearly anti-Christian bias. No longer would people look for answers in our institutions but would look elsewhere.

The Cable Age started in earnest in 1981 with the arrival of MTV, which would come to define the 1980s. MTV became the first of many networks who would embrace the new concept of narrowcasting. In the past, broadcast networks such as ABC and NBC aimed to capture a broad-based audience. MTV on the other hand was interested in only ages 12 to 24. Their primary focus was the youth culture.

Robert Pittman, Founder and Chairman of MTV, stated the following concerning MTV's philosophy, "We are dealing with a culture of TV babies. They can watch, do their home work, and listen to music all at the same time. And at MTV we don't shoot for 14 year olds, we own them. And the strongest appeal you can make is emotionally. If you can get their emotions going, they forget their logic. Then you've got them. They will accept almost anything over the screen. The only people that understand the new way to use that television set are the people who grew up with it."

Pittman summed up the entire Third Media Age in the above statement. First, there was a total commitment to reaching the youth culture. And second, there was an understanding and knowledge of the use of the television medium to captivate and hold audiences. Only those who grew up with television could fully understand how to use it effectively to reach audiences during the early days of cable television. MTV realized the power and the promise that television offered. If you understood how to use television effectively, you could control what the audience thought was important. And, by doing so, you could control their buying decisions.

MTV saw 14-year olds as their personal playground. Youth became nothing more than a possession to be controlled and manipulated. Just as the European powers in the 19th Century viewed Africa and Asia as a colony so did MTV view the youth culture. When you colonize a people group, you want to control their culture to implant your ideas and values and make it theirs. MTV and the media culture have done just that to our society. Their motivation was to gain power and control over the marketplace.

In MTV's world, everything was a form of advertising and marketing. That included the programming itself. MTV helped create an entire new model that was embraced by <u>all</u>

forms of media, including other television networks, TV studios, advertisers and news outlets.

Through very sophisticated marketing concepts, MTV learned how to eliminate the space that existed between entertainment, advertising, programming, branding, news, and marketing. These became indistinguishable from each other. MTV helped to establish the idea that marketing was more important than the program you were producing. Hollywood embraced this concept thoroughly at the beginning of the Third Media Age. The marketing of a film became more important than the film itself. Thanks to MTV, every form of media soon realized that the best way to maximize market share and to increase profit margin was to focus attention and resources on the marketing and selling of what a show or film represented rather than to concentrate on the programming itself or quality of the programming.

MTV branded a lifestyle. Embracing the products that appeared on MTV would enable the viewer to become the person he or she always wanted to be or to be like the models that appeared in the music videos. MTV encouraged viewers to embrace every aspect of celebrity, physical appearance and sexuality found in their programming.

This new form of marketing wasn't concerned about which products were best or about which products offered the best value. It was about ideas the products represented and how they would change your life. It helped you to identify with and embrace a lifestyle based on product use. For example, using a certain hair conditioner or shampoo meant you would be beautiful, popular, sexy and successful. Your life would have meaning and purpose because you were now the center of attention. Whether the shampoo made your hair look better was irrelevant. It was how the product made you feel about yourself and how others viewed you. But, can a shampoo really change your life? So what happens when we buy into the marketing and our life isn't changed? Of course, the next product will do the job because it's "new and improved".

Pittman also pointed out that the executives running MTV understood how to use television. After all, they were the first television generation. They grew up watching television. As their parents went off to work in the pursuit of the American Dream, the television set became their babysitter. And they learned well. In the early development of television in the 1950s, there were no experts. Most of the people who got involved in the industry really did not understand this new medium. But this new TV generation that grew up with it understood the keys to its success.

They learned the power of images and mythology or a belief system. Picture images can evoke deep emotions. They understood how to call up these deep emotions and memories that are buried deep inside of us. Today's image makers are using images to take on "new meanings" and have created new myths that are shrouded, often deliberately, by those deeper memories. They understood how to manipulate viewers to be good consumers. Their methods were psychologically driven and often very subtle. It's then that the viewer ends up buying the "idea" being sold by the image makers.

MTV spent millions of dollars to get into the minds of their audience. No television network or movie studio had ever done the type of research MTV did throughout the 1980s. MTV wanted to know how their audiences thought.

The end result was not to give their viewers the type of programs they wanted but to increase their ad revenues.

The Technology Explosion

The Third Media Age was characterized by an explosion of technological development. Cable television was made possible by advances in new telecommunication technologies developed during the space program. Without satellites orbiting the earth, cable television would not have been financially possible. Cable television offered up to 40 new channels. Today that number is well over 200 and growing. Many of the new channels embraced MTV's style of narrowcasting. It brought about an explosion of media choices. Cable networks were interested in finding a niche market, one that they could control and dominate. One of the reasons why marketing became such a powerful force during this time was because cable networks had to distinguish themselves from each other. Before the cable age, there were only three television networks. Marketing was not a concern because the viewer had few choices to consider. That all changed with the arrival of cable television and MTV.

Cable networks saw themselves as unique brands. The Weather Channel realized there was an audience for 24-hour weather coverage. CNN appealed to news junkies, while ESPN appealed to sports enthusiasts. Lifetime Network was only interested in women. History Channel appealed to history buffs. Each new cable network looked for its unique audience and developed programming to meet the needs and interests of their viewers.

During the late 1970s, the video cassette recorder (VCR) became available to the general public. The VCR revolutionized the way people viewed television and watched movies. Perhaps nothing has changed television more than the VCR. For the first time, viewers could determine what they wanted to watch and when they wanted to watch it. The VCR was the perfect companion to cable television.

Before the early 1980s, the only way you could see a movie was to go see it during it's theatrical release or wait three years to view an edited version on television. Thanks to the development of the VCR, the home video market was born. Movie viewing increased dramatically. If you wanted to see *Gone with the Wind*, it required only a visit to your local video store. With cable television and the availability of VCRs, television programs and unedited movies were available for viewing 24 hours a day, seven days a week.

In the 1950s, the American family gathered around a television set to watch their favorite programs. Now each family member had their own television set and would watch their own channel in the comfort of their own rooms. Hardly a healthy development. This helped to increase communication problems within the family that started during the Second Media Age. If television helped to unite us, cable television most certainly helped to divide us.

One of the most significant developments during this age was the creation of massive ownership groups. Media organizations were concentrated into powerful corporations. In the years following, five major media corporations have emerged, which control about 90% of media that is distributed in North America. Organizations such as News Corp., Disney, and CBS Corporation are a collection of movie studios, broadcast networks, cable interests, news outlets, internet, record labels and publishers. They had enormous power and the ability to move an artist, product, or project across a wide range of platforms. Most viewers are unaware that this is a form of advertising and marketing. For example, an individual could appear on a talk show, a television network and cable news program to promote his or her new movie or book. But most people don't realize they are owned by the same corporation.

As a result of the creation of these ownership groups, the few people that run these massive corporations are in a position to determine what you see and hear in the media. That includes both entertainment and news.

The media culture continued to grow in strength and size throughout the Third Media Age. Christian organizations embraced many of the principles that the media culture is based on. If you are embracing marketing, you are embracing the media culture. Christian organizations saw the benefits that media offered for potential growth and expansion. But without realizing it, is it possible that the marketing of Christianity became more important than Christianity itself? In the age of televangelists and Christian-based media ministries, the focus shifted away from God being the center of your life to selling a concept of what Christianity can do for you. For some ministries books, tapes, CDs and other merchandise became more important than the message. The idea that Christianity can make your life comfortable, safe and secure became more appealing than following the will of God, which does not guarantee your comfort. Was Christianity becoming just another marketing concept?

Marketing is the bridge that brings media and culture together. As the space continues to decrease between the two, they merge into one force. In other words, everything in culture becomes part of the marketplace. The media culture has played a part in creating a market-driven church where the emphasis is placed on the individual being satisfied with the products and services offered by the Church. Many in the church began to see the church as a brand to be promoted and marketed. These ideas were firmly planted during the 1980s and would be fully realized in the years ahead.

Finally, the Third Media Age led to a decentralization of media. There was no escape from its grasp and control of our society. Media was readily available with cable, broadcast, and video cassettes. Video images were everywhere from in-store to billboards. All this was intrusive, but it became a way of life.

The Fourth Media Age

Starting in 1997 with the wide availability of digital technology, we have now entered the Fourth Media Age or the Digital Age. This age is categorized by satellite television, cell phones, the internet, the DVD player, HD (high definition) television, social networking and mobile media devices. It is fueled by information and the need to connect and be part of something. When and where the media church started is a matter of debate. But it certainly found it's place in the Fourth Media Age.

George Miller, the director of Mel Gibson's Mad Max movies was quoted in 1998 as saying, "I believe cinema is now the most powerful secular religion. And people gather in cinemas to experience things collectively the way they once did in church. They are doing a lot of the work of our religious institutions, which have so concretized the metaphors in their stories, taken so much of the poetry, mystery and mysticism out of religious belief, that people look for other places to question their spirituality."

Miller offers insight into how and why the church of media and entertainment has grown quickly. Today's generation is asking questions and searching for spirituality. But they are not finding answers in the traditional church. But today's media, especially movies, is meeting the need for spirituality. Where the church has withdrawn from art, poetry and the mystery of life, Hollywood's screenwriters are more than willing to embrace the supernatural, mystery, mysticism and other forms of spirituality that can lead viewers to a new self-realization of truth.

Without question, this has helped to ignite and fuel the church of media and entertainment. There are also other forces at work that have helped define this new church. The process of change itself is a major contributing factor. We live in a time of uncertainty where we can no longer predict the future. Everything is in a constant state of flux. We are constantly moving and changing jobs. Even our relationships are unreliable. Information and knowledge continue to increase at a rapid pace. In five years, what is taught in school may be completely outdated. Our career choices may not exist in the next six months. Change will only accelerate in the years to come. We see everything in life constantly shifting and evolving.

So why shouldn't our beliefs or how we view God fit in this new way of life? It's impossible to believe that God is the same yesterday, today and forever in an ever-changing world. The only thing consistent or that makes sense is our media because we have control over it.

The growth of this church has been aided by a common language. This is the first generation that has grown up with the internet and social networking. They understand the language and are comfortable with building their own social networking sites. They also have an innate knowledge of computer skills. It is as if it is part of their DNA. Their language unites the church of media and entertainment. It is common ground where each member understands and recognizes the code.

The Fourth Media Age is defined by technology. There have always been technological advances, but this age is characterized by constant, rapid, and evolving technology. It seems like every month there is something new and exciting in the marketplace from iPods to iPhones to iPads. And every new product is a "must have" to the members of this church. As technology has evolved, it has led to lower prices and accessibility to more users. Today everyone under the age of 25 has some form of a mobile media device. For most people, it is impossible to go ten minutes without texting, checking messages or surfing the web. There is a need to be constantly plugged in and accessible to one's media.

This media church is most certainly defined by its lifestyle. They have a constant need for connectivity, social networking and creativity. They are just as likely to watch media as they are to create it. YouTube has become their new playground. In fact, it is more real than life itself. In some ways, the media they create and distribute is not only a reflection of who they are, but it becomes a way of life that defines their lifestyle.

The Digital Age has defined this new church of media and entertainment and has created a personal value system for each to its members. Those who have come of age during this time have sought experiences that give their lives meaning. They are looking for a personal, custom-made, virtual world that they can create by their media choices that defines who they are. It is here that they find value, purpose and an experience that is outside of themselves.

The Fourth Media Age is heavily influenced by the philosophy of postmodernism. Where modernism had answers in science, postmodernism says there are no answers or absolutes. And no one belief system can explain the origins or meaning of life. Your truth or your understanding is only relevant to you and may not work for others. This philosophy has been thoroughly embraced by every form of media in the past few years. Where the Third Media Age may have had a clearly antiChristian bias, this age is more than willing to accept Christian philosophy. The problem is that Christianity is being blended into every other world philosophy or world religion.

Since postmodernism teaches there are no absolute truths, you are left in a position to pick and choose. In other words, create your own philosophy or theology that works for you. Could we be in the process of creating a new gospel, a new form of Christianity? Could that be the ultimate outcome of the Fourth Media Age?

It's impossible not to talk about the impact that the DVD player has had in this age. The DVD player is the world's most successful electronic device to date. It has revolutionized the way we watch movies. Its development caused a massive explosion in home video. Some studios decided to bypass theatrical distribution and go straight to video. This has lead to an increase in production of hundreds of films yearly that otherwise would not have been produced. Today, the average person will view at least 40 movies per year. That number is substantially higher for those under the age of 25. Movies have become a part of the fabric of life.

Another major development of this age is social networking. We have a need to connect. But the very thing we seek, we may lose. This new technology may be having the opposite affect. It's allowing us the opportunity to stay behind the keyboard and create the kind of message that we want to communicate to others. We can be whoever we want to be without ever having to face an individual. In this new world, we are in total control. It allows us to have social contact without really communicating.

It is just like Marshall McLuhan said in his book, *Understanding Media, the Extensions of Man.* McLuhan believed the medium **was** the message. He stated that television would have consequences and would change behavior patterns in ways we would not understand for years. In the same way, social media and the technologies of the internet will also have consequences that we do not understand today.

A Single Story Arc

Over the past few decades, we have seen a series of seemingly random events leading to "A Perfect Storm", which has created a powerful media culture. Do we have a single story arc that has emerged from today's media? Has this story arc directly or indirectly through our mass media been institutionalized in our culture?

As I stated earlier, business, media and culture have combined to create a unique relationship, which is based on the pursuit of consumerism. This story arc is about convincing YOU that you are more important than anything. Your wants, needs and desires are your first priority and must be met at any cost. This keeps YOU as a good consumer. Any threat to this concept will disrupt the current system. Today's media culture does not deny the existence of God nor does it tell us not to believe in him, but it does allow us to the opportunity to put ourselves at the center of our lives. For Christians, the media culture has helped us to create an image of God that fits into our lifestyle. By doing that, we can pursue our own goals and objectives without feeling guilty.

I fully understand this message is not new. It has been around since the fall of man. It is our basic instincts, our worst nature. What is different today is the scope and size of the massive media culture which has been created over the past few years. Its ability to focus a message with enormous power is undeniable. Not every television program or movie will directly communicate this message, but most often it will be conveyed in subtext or some other subconscious means.

Consider the following facts. The average person will have watched 18,000 hours of television and viewed 320,000 30-sec commercial ads before the age of 18. That's compared to only 12,000 hours in the classroom. It becomes a numbers game with the right images over a long enough period of time through many different platforms, such as movies, TV, web, and advertising. The media culture will find a way to get this message across that YOU are the center of the universe, and YOU are more important than anything else, guaranteed.

In 1956, the President of Indonesia had the opportunity to talk to some of the key Hollywood executives of the day. He stated that he regarded them as political radicals and political revolutionaries, who had hastened political change in the East (creating unrest). What the Orient saw in a Hollywood movie was a world in which all the ordinary people had cars, electrical stoves, and refrigerators. Now the Orient regards itself as the ordinary person who has been deprived of the ordinary man's birthright.

Today, cars and appliances are commonplace in our culture. But what do we consider today to be "our" birthright? What is the media culture telling us WE deserve? Whether intentional or not, media has helped create an environment in which YOU have the right to have everything you want. For Christians this created a paradox. We understand that the Bible teaches us to put God first. But the media culture communicates an entirely different message. We struggle to balance the two. But often we fail because we do not understand the complex pressures that the media culture exerts.

The Rise of Business

In Ron Luce's book, *Battlecry for a Generation, the Fight to Save America's Youth*, he states that our culture is now dominated by business. He goes on to point out that the world had been ruled by tribes, armies, religion, and politics. Today, since the fall of the Berlin Wall, business now rules the world. He goes on to point out that we now have a particularly subversive mantra. Luce says, "If I have the ability to make money at something, then I have the right to do it." He believes that the ugly flipside of this is that it allows for no objective moral compass to guide our business institutions. And that includes the relationship that now exists between media and business. As long as the viewers keep buying the products, the networks, media or business interests will do whatever it takes to keep us infatuated with the images and messages that they communicate.

I am not suggesting that business is necessarily bad. Nor am I trying to communicate that capitalism should be abolished. But I do believe our current system is out of balance. There is nothing wrong with owning a home, wanting what is best for your family or making a profit. But, unfortunately, it has become an obsession with no moral compass to guide us. We now are in a culture that not only needs to make a profit but must maximize profits by all means.

Our new golden rule could be stated that making money is not only your right but is your responsibility and duty no matter what the cost. It certainly helps to explain some of the recent headlines such as runaway greed on Wall Street and the abuses in our banking industry. I'm not sure if it is about the money or what the money can do for you. Somehow having the money proves your worth as a human being in our society. It's fueled by a distortion of the American Dream.

Today, society believes they deserve everything they want. They believe it is their right no matter what it takes or whatever they have to do to get what they want. For example, if you can make 10% profit why not 20%. If you can make 20% profit, why not 40% and so on. It helps to explain why American businesses are willing to close down factories and send millions of jobs overseas. It explains risky loans and bad investments.

It has turned us all into good consumers, who will work at whatever it takes to achieve the American Dream even at the expense of our families. It also puts every social ill in perspective whether directly or indirectly. Influenced by this relationship between media and business, our nation has suffered through serious problems. How else can we explain depression, teen suicide, drug and alcohol dependency, violence, and a host of other problems.

The Perfect Storm Has Formed

The perfect storm has formed, and we are living it. The four media ages that our nation has experienced have brought us to a crossroads. We have created a culture that USA Today in 1998 coined "the toxic culture". It's toxic to everything it touches. Every idea or thought is distorted. Nowhere is this more apparent than in the relationship that exists between media and business. We need to restore some sense of balance and perspective. The American Dream needs to be redefined. But how do we do that? I don't claim to have all the answers. I have tried to put some of the pieces together.

From my research, I have concluded that the American Dream has been perverted, and consumerism is the root cause of many of our social ills. Most of all, I believe media is the prime driving force within our society.

Appendix 2   The Power of Film

I often talk about the power of film. I'm convinced that movies are the most unique form of all media. There is something remarkably different about the effectiveness and impact of a movie compared to television shows, video games, web content or any other type of electronic image. In fact, film transcends all other forms of media. That means movies have a unique place and influence in our society. It's through films that we can express our wants, fears, hurts and desires. Cinema has a unique ability to shape public perception while educating and enlightening our society. There is no question that movies have changed our perceptions and influenced and impacted the very fabric of culture and our nation. Movies challenge us individually to consider our lifestyle choices as well as the pathway we are currently pursuing.

So why do movies have this unique ability more than other media forms? What makes them different? Why are they more capable of communicating powerful messages?

What separates the film experience from all other forms of media?

1. The cinematic experience. There is something very different and profound about entering a dark theater. It is perhaps the only place that we truly shut out the outside world. Where else do drop off of the planet for two hours. No cell phones, beepers or electronic media devices allowed. When most of us go on vacation, we check our e-mails. Movies at the theatrical level have our total, undivided attention. If we are spending ten bucks, most of us want to get our money's worth. We are not in control of the cinematic experience. We cannot hit pause or rewind. We are totally immersed in both sound and image. There is nothing like the big screen because it creates an experience more real in some ways than life itself.

2. Movies are about something. A few years ago, I heard an industry insider say that movies are about something or at least the good ones are. He is absolutely right. Films are not like television shows or web-based content because they are typically anywhere from 90 to 120 minutes in length. In other words, you have to have something of importance to drive two hours of content. Plot will not get it done. Movies require a theme. The characters must need something in order for movies to work on an emotional and psychological level. Movies work best with big ideas such as justice, forgiveness, redemption, freedom, social change, philosophy, or political change. Movies work on a big canvas so they require something important to say in order to hold our attention and

interest. Why do films such as *Casablanca, Citizen Kane* or the *Wizard of Oz* hold up after all of these years? Because they were all about something. *Wizard of Oz* had two themes: (1) finding your way back home and (2) the thing you seek the most, you always had it within your possession. Those are universal themes that are just as relevant today as they were at the time these movies were produced.

3. The group experience. Where else do we gather with total strangers to share an experience such as viewing a film? We laugh together, cry together and are frightened together. There is something powerful about a group experience. It validates the importance of the message that a film expresses. Since we usually see films with friends and family, a good or challenging movie always invites a discussion such as, "How did the movie impact you? What did you think about this character or that particular scene? Did you understand what the movie was about?" What other forms of media can you think about where we have this kind of profound discussion and dialogue?

4. The journey. All films are part of a journey. Movies most often are about the human condition. What makes us human? Films have the capability of taking us on this journey as we seek answers. We can relate to this because at some level we are all on our own personal journey trying to make sense of the world we live in. It's expressed through what writers call the "character's arc". Films can transcend both space and time. In fact, we can see a character's entire lifespan in a film. Through this

process we can see how characters change and whether they are moving toward the truth or away from the truth. We can witness a conflict of values as characters wrestle with their inner demons to move from vice to virtue. Movies are the only form of media that has the ability to present this type of character arc and development. Through this process, we can see our lives played out in the characters portrayed on the big screen.

5. The suspension of reality. When does a movie stop being fiction and take on the form of reality? If the filmmakers have done their job well, there is a point at which the audience crosses a threshold where they start to believe what they see in a movie is reality. It's no longer a film but a reflection of the real world. I'm convinced that film is the only form of media that can do this convincingly. I'm sure you know what I'm talking about when a movie has the ability to transport us to a different time, age, world, or even a different universe. Can you think of a film where the experience became so real that you forgot you were watching a movie? When this happens, truth can be communicated on a very deep, personal level. You care very deeply about the characters, their fates and their causes. You can imagine how God can use this experience in our lives to reflect his glory and truth.

Appendix 3   The Movies

Smoke Signals

It's interesting to see how well a movie holds up over time. Is it still relevant? Does it speak to the current generation? Or is it forever trapped in the past, out of step, unable to relate to the current times? I recently watched one of my favorite films from 1998, Smoke Signals, and I asked myself those same questions. Watching this movie again reinforced my belief that Smoke Signals deserved all the acclaim it received.

Smoke Signals had won several awards that year, at the Sundance Film Festival, including Best Picture. It transcends time with a universal message that is just as relevant today. It was the first feature movie written, directed, and acted entirely by Native Americans. It offers a fascinating perspective on Native American culture rarely seen in today's media. And it's done through humor as Native Americans are poking fun at themselves. "It's a good day to be indigenous", as the weather report says on the reservation radio station KREZ.

Smoke Signals not only helps Native Americans to better understand themselves but also transcends culture and speaks to all of us. The director, Chris Eyre, describes the movie as a "universal story about fathers and friends and forgiveness". The story centers around two 20-year-old, modern day Coeur d'alene Indians, Victor Joseph (Adam Beach) and Thomas Builds-the-Fire (Evan Adams), who leave their Idaho reservation to retrieve the ashes of Victor's father, Arnold (Gary Farmer), in Arizona.

Victor and Thomas have nothing in common, but they are linked together through their relationship with Victor's father. Victor has a somewhat ambiguous relationship with Thomas as he is trying to understand his friend's pain. Along their way, they are presented several challenges that lead them to discover life's meaning and possibilities. This film is a road movie, and I love road movies. It's never about getting to the destination. The journey is always a metaphor for something greater. The real story is what happens to Victor and Thomas on their journey.

Will they unlock their past? Can they develop a friendship? And what about life's big question, "Are we willing to forgive and move on?" Smoke Signals is an honest film willing to take a hard look at Native American culture. It allows the viewer insights into the world it portrays. The movie deals with alcoholism and the quiet anger of the outside world that surrounds the reservation. But the movie also celebrates Native American traditions such as oratorical storytelling. Fry bread is used several times in the film and serves as a vehicle to introduce Christian elements into the story as Thomas tells Victor, "It is used for communion".

It's an interesting mix of Christian symbolism and Native American traditions.

I especially enjoyed the witty and poignant dialogue. I have to warn you that this is a talking movie. It's all about "the story" so don't expect any action sequences. The film goes back and forth between two time periods that are woven together with seamless flashbacks.

Smoke Signals is a very spiritual film that I think could change the way you think about forgiveness. Victor asks, "How do we forgive our fathers? Maybe in a dream. Do we forgive our fathers in our age or theirs? Or in their deaths. Saying it to them or not saying it."

We are all on a journey to forgive someone as we seek our own forgiveness. Smoke Signals is available on DVD for less than $10 at most online stores. It is highly recommended.

The Mighty

Sometimes life can be hard and unfair. I'm sure that's how the filmmakers for The Mighty must have felt. Released in 1998, The Mighty is a comedy drama based on the book, Freak the Mighty, by Rodman Philbrick. It went on to receive strong reviews and was considered one of the best films of the year. Amazingly, it was a huge commercial flop for Miramax Films. Was it the marketing? Lack of marketing? Bad Luck?

At the time, Miramax was the hottest studio in Hollywood. Everything they touched turned to gold with big hits like *The English Patient* and *Goodwill Hunting*. In fact, The Mighty was considered to be the next *Goodwill Hunting*, which helped to launch the careers of Matt Damon and Ben Affleck.

The Mighty has so much going for it. It is an enduring story with a whimsical and magical feel. It has an excellent cast and a wonderful sound track, featuring a song from Sting. The Mighty deserved a better fate. Today, it is mostly forgotten. But it is a lost treasure worth discovering.

The Mighty is a welcome change from movies that typically portray teens doing the wrong things and embracing bad lifestyle choices. It is a positive and uplifting movie that speaks to our ability to overcome physical and emotional handicaps through the power of friendship. They discover an inner strength that lies within us all. The Mighty does this without resorting to ridiculous comics or unbelievable, happy-ending nonsense.

The Mighty is a story about two boys who are social outcasts. Both are tormented and bullied by Blake and his teenage gang. Max (Eldon Henson) is physically strong but suffers from a learning disability called dyslexia. Kevin (Kieran Culkin) is physically weak from his battle with morquio syndrome. He is extremely intelligent and creative. They form an unlikely alliance, and together they are able to do the impossible. "You need a brain. I need legs, and the Wizard of Oz doesn't live in South Cincinnati", exclaimed Kevin to Max. Through their symbiotic friendship, they are able to balance out their strengths and weaknesses to complete one person. Soon they are on a quest as knights in King Arthur's Court to rescue fair maidens, slay dragons and walk high above the world. Back in the real world, they face more challenges from Blake and his gang to problems at school and at home, including the impending release of Max's father from prison.

Are we defined by our past or our parents mistakes? Kevin teaches Max that a Knight proves his worthiness through his deeds. This is one of the strongest themes that runs throughout The Mighty. We also see that through a nonviolent approach, we can right injustices and defend the rights of the weak. I consider The Mighty to be a very spiritual film because we are all on a quest in one way or another.

Rounding out the cast are wonderful performances by Sharon Stone as Kevin's mom along with veteran actor, Harry Dean Stanton (he always bring his A game) as Grim, Max's grandfather. In minor roles are X-Files' Gillian Anderson, who is almost unrecognizable as Loretta Lee and James Gandolfini (The Sopranos) as Kenny (Killer) Cain.

The Mighty could have been your typical family film or even the dreaded after-school special. And it could have floundered in cheap sentimentality. But, under the steady direction of Peter Chelson, the film found a balance between fantasy and reality.

Kevin and Max live in a gritty, urban environment full of poverty and despair. The film has a realistic feel. You might call it an edgy, family film with an intelligent story. It explores many themes typically not found in the family film genre, including strength of character, acceptance, self-worth and identity.

So what are you watching Friday or Saturday night? The same old typical Hollywood special effects bonanza? How about considering a movie with some substance that will inspire you, challenge you to be a better person, or make you feel how special life can be. You probably won't find The Mighty for rent, but it is available online for under $10. Check out deepdiscount.com. Inspiration and courage can be found in the most unlikely places.

The Spitfire Grill

A couple of nights ago, I screened The Spitfire Grill, a film from 1996, for my media class. Why would I pick a 14-year old, relatively unknown movie when there are plenty of new movies available? Because I'm looking for something special, something unique, and something often not found. I found a gem with The Spitfire Grill. Yes, it's the kind of movie that Christians and media missionaries should be making, a redemptive story with heart and an emotional impact.

It fits my definition of a Christian film without being a "Christian" film, and it does so by speaking about Jesus the least but having him most in mind. There are so few movies that accomplish this. It's a true balancing act. There are a couple of other examples that come to mind, such as *To End All Wars* and *Bella*.

What do all of these films have in common? They all deal with pain and the human condition, which can be ugly at times. But somehow, they are also a celebration of life. They don't pull their punches. They all have an emotional impact. They offer believable dialogue with believable characters. They are not afraid to use symbolism or metaphors. They understand that you have the intelligence to figure it out on your own. They don't feel contrived or manipulated. That means the screenwriter isn't throwing a bunch of plot points together to fulfill his or her agenda. All of these films offer no easy answers or any fairytale ending. But, above all, they are honest and truthful.

The Spitfire Grill exceeds at all of these points. It is redemptive filmmaking at its best. The story is about a young girl recently released from prison. Percy Talbott, played by Alison Elliott, is looking for a fresh start. She arrives in a small town in Maine with hopes of starting a new life. She finds work at the Spitfire Grill owned by Hannah, played my veteran actress Helen Bursteyn.

As the story unfolds, we soon discover Percy's tragic past. We also realize that Gilead, her new home, is a town with no future and no hope. Do we get second chances? And can we forgive ourselves for our past mistakes? These are the questions that the characters in Spitfire Grill must wrestle with.

The Spitfire Grill debuted at the Sundance Film Festival in 1996. It won the prestigious Audience Award for best narrative film. The film was acquired by Castle Rock Entertainment for $10 million, which at the time was the highest amount paid for any independent feature film.

I find it amazing that The Spitfire Grill was able to have so much success at Sundance. To say the least, the audience that attends the festival is somewhat diverse. Obviously, they did not see this as a Christian film. It was only later that critics pointed out that the funding for the film came from a Christian-based ministry. That criticism killed what could have been a much larger audience for the film.

Sacred Heart League, a Roman Catholic, non-profit communications organization based in Mississippi, put up the funding of $6 million to make The Spitfire Grill. They looked at over 200 perspective screenplays looking for work that embraced Judeo-Christian values and good storytelling. They found what they were looking for in The Spitfire Grill.

It took real guts to do what they did, putting $6 million in play with no hope of any return. They had no distribution deal until they got to Sundance. But, more importantly, they weren't looking just to make a "Christian" film. They had the courage to take chances and allow the material to breathe.

I hope you take the time to discover The Spitfire Grill. It's a journey worth taking. It's available currently on DVD. Because of its age, it's unlikely you will be able to rent it. But I have found some online sources where it is available for as little as $6. Do yourself a favor and buy it.

Places in the Heart

How many movies do you think have been made since Al Jolson's *The Jazz Singer* in 1927, which by the way was the first talking film? 5,000? 10,000? 20,000? Perhaps no one has an exact count. But I would put the number between 30,000 – 40,000 movies. So, would you agree, that's a lot of films?

It would be very easy to overlook movies that we should not forget. One of these films is from 1984, Places in the Heart. Again, this is another example of the type of movies that Christians should be making. An exceptional film of rare beauty, simplicity and grace, Places in the Heart weaves Christian themes into a masterpiece that tells all of us that God's love and forgiveness is available to all who accept it, both good and evil, black or white, and young or old.

The movie will undoubtedly surprise you, especially the ending. There is more going on than what's occurring on the surface. Could Places in the Heart be a metaphor for something else? But what? The screenplay is based on writer/director Robert Benson's childhood memories of growing up in Waxahachie, Texas during the depression era of the 1930s. Benson is successful in taking us on a journey to experience a different time, place and people. It is a rare look at pure Americana. The filmmakers are magnificent at recreating an authentic, historical representation of Texas during the depression. I've seen a lot of movies that have attempted this that, quite frankly, look fake. Places in the Heart is the real deal.

The general story goes something like this. Edna Spalding portrayed by Sally Field is struggling to save her home after her husband is accidently killed. Along the way, she must overcome hardships and struggles in bringing in the first cotton harvest of the season. She forms a surrogate family, including Mr. Will (John Malkovich), a blind boarder who sees what others cannot see, and Moze (Danny Glover) an African-American sharecropper whose wisdom helps Edna save the farm.

There is also a subplot involving an adulterous triangle, which threatens to destroy two marriages. Together our characters face bigotry and racial hatred and must overcome their fears, survive life's hardships and learn to forgive.

Places in the Heart was nominated for five Academy Awards and took home two Oscars. Sally Field won Best Actress, and Robert Benson won Best Original Screenplay. Some of you may find this film a bit slow by today's standards. It's unquestionably a character study. And, sure, the storyline is a little simplistic. But it is the end of the film that makes the journey worth the effort. It's at this point that you realize why these characters went through the hardships they had to endure. You see their reward and the simplicity of abiding love.

Some critics claim the overall narrative of the film does not support such a powerful and compelling conclusion. They are absolutely mistaken. They fail to understand that life isn't always about huge events. But it's the small things in everyday life that define us.

If you haven't seen Places in the Heart or, like me, you haven't seen it in 20 years, it's definitely worth a look. It's available on DVD. On most sites you can pick it up for less than $10. If you want to experience a different time, place and people, I can't think of a better journey than Places in the Heart.

Lars and the Real Girl

This is one of those films that is off the beaten path. Independent cinema offers a voice not heard in mainstream Hollywood. It can be the best place to find spiritual films. Perhaps independent filmmakers have more creative freedom and expression than their mainstream counterparts in Hollywood.

It does require some effort and time to discover these "little" films that often get overlooked. But it's worth the journey. All that is necessary is a little discernment and a taste for the unusualness and quirkiness of life, which we all possess.

I've seen Lars and the Real Girl several times, and with each viewing I discover something new, which is usually a sign of a great film. This is a beautifully made film. Filmmaking can be a difficult process, but when everything comes together, you have magic. In the case of Lars and the Real Girl, we have a director with a clear vision, a writer who has written a powerful screenplay, and the right actors who have been appropriately cast for difficult parts. Plus, the cinematography is first class.

I find it interesting when writers choose quirky little Midwestern towns in the dead of winter for their backdrop. The filmmakers are successful in making the town an intricate character in the story. But the most enduring elements of the film are sense of community, acceptance, love and kindness. Lars and the Real Girl is a spiritual film because of its reflection of what a true Christian community should be. I'm not sure that's what the filmmakers had in mind, but that's what they've created.

The film is a reflection of I John 3:18, which says, "My little children, let us not love in word, neither in tongue, but in deed and in truth." The town folks in Lars and the Real Girl are challenged to put their faith and love into action. In other words, it's a practical application of what they believe. What we have here is another example of a "Christian" film that's not a Christian film. If you are interested in making movies from a faith-based perspective, I highly recommend that you take a look at this film from several different angles to break down each element and discover why it works.

Here's a quick synopsis. Lars Lindstrom (Ryan Gosling) is a lonely, shy and socially inept young man living in the converted garage behind the house of his brother and sister-in-law. Lars develops a relationship with a life-like doll that is anatomically correct, which he orders on-line from an adult website. I know it sounds creepy, but this is a case where the content makes complete sense in terms of the context of the film. So don't freak out. Lars has detached from reality and is convinced that Bianca (the life-sized doll) is a real person. In fact, she is a wheelchair-bound missionary from Brazil.

Lars' brother, Gus, and sister-in-law, Karin, convince Lars to take Bianca to see the family doctor, who is also a psychologist. Her diagnosis is that this is a delusion of Lars own creation and urges Gus and Karen to treat Bianca as if she is a real person.

So how do Gus and Karin handle the situation? How will the church they regularly attend react? What about the townsfolk's? Will they go along? Can anybody help Lars?

For some, this plot may seem preposterous and implausible. But somewhere along the way, the filmmakers find the divine that exists in each of us through God's grace and love. It's a clear question of how far we are willing to go in reaching out to people in need even those different from us. Can we get out of our comfort zone? We, as Christians, love the idea of Christianity and often practice our faith as theory. But, at times, we have difficulty putting it into action. Without action or deed, our faith really doesn't mean much.

We find in Lars and the Real Girl the real Christian community that we all hope for—unconditional love, acceptance and redemption. How can we make our current Christian community reflect a true Biblical community? How can I reach out in love to people that I don't understand and find different than me? Am I willing to go the distance no matter the personal cost, including looking ridiculous.

Like Lars, on some level, we have all disconnected perhaps from God and each other. How can we find our way back? What was Lars turning point? Is there something from Lars and the Real Girl that I can apply to my personal life?

To End All Wars

To End All Wars takes us to places where other war films have no interest in exploring. The film was written by Brian Godawa and may be his best work to-date. It is one of the best examples of a truly redemptive film that has come out in the past few years. In fact, it could serve as the poster child for the type of films that Christians and media missionaries should be making. It offers a profound message without being overtly preachy. Powerful doesn't even begin to describe its impact. The screenplay is based on the autobiography of Ernest Gordan and recounts his story as a prisoner of war in Thailand during World War II.

But the story is really not a war movie. Most of us are familiar with the historical details of the construction of the Burma railroad and the cruelties of the Japanese captors as told in the movie, *The Bridge on the River Kwai*, but this is the part of the story that you don't know.

The story centers around Ernest Gordan, played by Ciaran McMenamin, who is recovering from a near fatal disease. He begins to teach his fellow prisoners philosophy from Plato and Shakespeare, along with teachings from the Bible. Gordan's superior officer, Major Ian Campbell, played by Robert Carlye, is critical of the increasing pacifist teachings of Gordan. Also skeptical is Jim Reardon, the lone American, played by Keifer Sutherland. Reardon also runs a black market on the side and is interested only in self-preservation.

How do we remain human under such inhuman conditions? Is it possible to keep our faith? To End All Wars explores these questions as well as other difficult philosophic and moral issues. These prisoners are caught in the trap of hate and vengeance toward the Japanese. Do they find a way out? Are we truly our brother's keeper? Under the relentless conditions of brutality in the camp, can the soldiers learn to survive and find the meaning and purpose from Gordan's teachings?

Yes, there is brutality and, at times, it can be difficult to watch. However, it offers a positive and hopeful message that somehow humans are capable of finding their humanity, even under the most brutal conditions. This film should be required viewing for all future media missionaries. It is impossible to watch and not be moved through great feelings of pain as well as joy.

Released in 2001 by 20th Century Fox, To End All Wars deserved a larger audience. Screened at the Toronto Film Festival as an official selection, the film received positive reviews. It is currently available on DVD.

Bella

Bella is the type of movie I wish more filmmakers would embrace. It is a beautiful story full of life, grace and hope. Bella is a classic example of the power of God at work in film and media. If you are both a Christian and a filmmaker, this movie should inspire you to make films that can illustrate God's glory and truth at work in the world. Bella accomplishes both goals of revealing God's glory and truth without being preachy or judgmental. This is an enormous accomplishment, especially for a first-time filmmaker.

Director, Alejándro Gomez Monteverde, illustrates enormous skill in creating a near perfect film. He undoubtedly has a keen sense of how to relate to audiences with material that speaks to the heart. The story is authentic, real and compelling.

The film starts out with one of the most profound and insightful narrations I have ever heard in any film. If you want to make God laugh, tell him your plans. Without giving away too much of the basic story elements, Bella tells the stories of José (Eduardo Verástegui), who is a Manhattan chef at an elegant Mexican restaurant and Nina (Tammy Blanchard), who is a waitress facing a difficult crisis. After Nina is fired for being late for work, Jose leaves his job, and they both embark on a journey throughout New York City, which ultimately leads to the home of José's parents on Long Island.

Nina is forced to make a difficult decision after revealing to Jose that she is pregnant and considering an abortion. Jose has his own past demons to deal with as well. The story structure is told out of sequence so the audience never completely understands what is occurring. But the heart of Bella is about redemption and forgiving ourselves for our past mistakes.

Bella is successful at combining low-budget and independent film concepts and ideas with a strong transformational story arc. The film won the prestigious People's Choice Award at the 2006 Toronto International Film Festival. Bella tackles a very touchy subject of abortion and the sanctity of life. As evident to its victory at Toronto, the film found a balance in speaking to a mainstream audience about a difficult subject. It did it in a fashion that was not preachy but offered an honest view of how God views the importance of life. One of the main reasons why I like the film is because it felt real and genuine in its ability to embrace life to it's fullest.

Bella has a way of transforming the small moments of everyday existence into divine encounters with God's grace. Bella is a celebration of the joys of family with all of its complications and difficulties. It reminds us that the importance of love is always the unifying and defining element that binds us together. The ending is especially fulfilling. Most writers would have taken the easy way out and offered up the typical Hollywood romantic ending. But we are left with embracing an ending that offers hope but that doesn't always tie up every loose end. There is an energy and excitement in this film, thanks in part to the depiction of a culture that we normally do not see in the movies.

Bella reflects the rich culture of the Hispanic community in America. It is a refreshing insight and perspective into the lives of immigrants and their children living as first-generation Americans. The film was shot on location in New York City. The director, Alejándro Gomez Monteverde, was determined to shoot on location because he believed it was essential to the story. The city provided the necessary ambiance to make Bella feel rich with the essence of life. There is no better film that celebrates life so richly as Bella. It is an artistic masterpiece that serves as one of the best examples for Christians who are called to make films as media missionaries.

Sweet Land

Small movies are often the best stories because they represent a filmmaker's personal journey and experiences in life. One of these films is from 2006 called Sweet Land. You have probably never heard of it. It's usually one of those unknown titles that you see on critics' top ten film lists. You ask yourself, how did I miss this one? Sweet Land was named one of the best films in 2006 in both *Entertainment Weekly* and *Los Angeles Times* top ten lists. Most films like Sweet Land never receive wide distribution because they are independently produced and have limited and inadequate resources for distribution. That is a shame because Sweet Land is one film that is worth the effort to find.

The film is set in the early 1920s in rural Minnesota and is based on Will Weber's 1989 short story, "A Gravestone Made of Wheat". Sweet Land is basically an old-fashioned, romance story, the kind of movie Hollywood used to make. Inge Atenberg, played by Elizabeth Reaser, is an independent, feisty German mail-order bride who travels to Minnesota to marry Olaf Torvik, played by Tim Geinee, a young Norwegian immigrant farmer. The people of the Minnesota farming community are openly hostile toward Inge because of her German heritage. To make matters worse, the local minister refused to marry the couple because they did not have the proper papers. There are also further complications because the town's banker is trying to foreclose on Olaf's farm. With no support or help from the community, what will the couple do?

Sweet Land offers an interesting and historical look at an often forgotten part of our history. What does it truly mean to be an American? How do we overcome our prejudice? The film is a labor of love. First time filmmaker, Ali Selim, spent over 15 years trying to get this film made. Nobody in Hollywood was interested in making the film. In fact, he raised over a million dollars to produce the film himself, mostly from private investors in Minnesota.

Sweet Land is also a very spiritual film. You won't find a better example of two scenes that illustrate the difference between the indifference of religion and what a relationship with God really looks like. It is a refreshing change of pace when the town's local Lutheran minister realizes that true belief can be expressed in a multitude of ways.

Sweet Land was also honored with an Independent Spirit Award for Best First Feature. What also makes the film stand out is the beauty and simplicity of its cinematography. In fact, the Minnesota countryside is as much a character in the film as Inge and Olaf. It's rare that independent films have the ability to adequately recreate an authentic, historical representation of the past.

Sweet Land also offers a strong sense of purpose. The characters are destined and determined to build a life and a place for their children and descendents. They played a part in building our nation. Sweet Land is a celebration of the immigrant spirit and determination to overcome and to endure. If you are looking for something different than the usual mainstream, Hollywood fare, then Sweet Land offers a detour into a time and place that will reenergize your passion for life. It's an opportunity to reconnect to our heritage and our land.

The Book of Eli

I see a lot of movies. Probably too many. But it's part of my ministry trying to make sense of the media and what movies are communicating to us. Most are forgettable and, quite honestly, a waste of my time and yours. But that's not the case with The Book of Eli. It's one of the best films I have seen in a long time.

All good movies have one thing in common. They are about something. And they offer substance. The Book of Eli takes place in a post-apocalyptic world in the near future. It is not your typical Mad Max movie. Lately, we have had a rash of end-of-the-world films such as *2012* and *Knowing*. Some people believe that with the approaching end of the Mayan calendar in December of 2012 that catastrophic events will occur on earth.

The Book of Eli obviously plays on our fears of the unknown and of a possible bleak future. But this film not only portrays the future as a desolate wasteland but offers hope of a new tomorrow based on God's everlasting truth. The film is a classic example of a Christian movie that is not a "Christian" movie. There is no doubt that The Book of Eli offers a Christian message, but it does it in an authentic, honest and truthful manner.

The Book of Eli was not made by a Christian company nor were most of the people involved Christians. We could learn a thing or two from nonbelievers about the art of filmmaking. The Book of Eli does not commit the fatal mistake of having an agenda or preaching a message before the importance of telling a compelling story. The characters drive the story, and you never feel like you are being manipulated.

The basic story goes something like this: Denzel Washington plays the role of Eli, a mysterious stranger who wanders the desolate highways of a post-apocalyptic world. He must fight off blood-thirsty gangs in a lawless civilization as he is on a quest to protect a mysterious book as he moves westward. Gary Oldman plays the role of the antagonist, Carnegie, who is bent on possessing the book for his own purposes. He tells Eli, "I grew up with it. I know its power, and if you read it so do you." Apparently the world has gone through some type of war, and there is a hole in the atmosphere. The surviving people are fighting for the little remaining resources. They blamed religion for the war and have destroyed every Bible except one. Eli has the last surviving Bible on the face of the earth. He is on a God-given quest, a journey of faith. He has been given the mission to protect the Word of God and bring it to a place of safety where it once again can be printed.

There are so many reasons why I love this movie. The Book of Eli makes you think about the importance of the Word of God. What if it was lost, and people forgot about its meaning? The film places a new value and importance on actually reading the book. The first thing I thought was maybe I should read the Bible more. I'm not sure I've seen a better example of a movie that portrays a character who walks by faith and listens to the voice of God. Remember, this is a mainstream, commercial film produced by Warner Brothers Pictures. It made over $95 million at the box office.

In several interviews, Denzel Washington, who is a committed Christian, said he had a substantial hand in tweaking the script, and it shows in the end result. The core message of this film is God is in control. Even if the world is in total chaos, God's Word will go forward and replicate. Mila Kunis plays Solara, the daughter of Carnegie, who actually becomes the first convert and carries on Eli's mission.

Denzel Washington and Gary Oldman do an outstanding job in their roles. Washington may be the best actor in his generation, and Oldman may be the best character actor we have seen in a long time. Every element in this film is outstanding. The cinematography is breathtaking considering they are portraying an apocalyptic world. Every shot is well constructed and has a purpose. The music score is haunting and, quite frankly, hypnotic.

The Book of Eli is not for everyone. Obviously, I do not consider it to be family-friendly entertainment. This film is meant for a mature audience because it does contain a fair amount of graphic violence and bad language. But I believe these are essential to the authentic nature of the film. Eli's violent nature serves to protect the Book at all costs. But as he reads the Book, he is transformed more and more as he applies it to his life. Some people may object to the notion that the Word of God can be used in a negative fashion because Carnegie plans on using the Word to control and manipulate people that he feels are feeble-minded and weak. But, unfortunately, our history points to the fact that the Word of God has been used for both good and bad.

If you are looking for a movie about something, especially something important, you will do no better than seeing The Book of Eli. It is a film that you will not forget. I am personally convinced that we need movies that make us think about the things that are really important. The Book of

Eli does this and more. You can find it on DVD and Blu-ray disc. This is one journey worth taking.

Henry Poole is Here

I always enjoy movies that explore challenging subject material, especially matters of faith, doubts and unbelief. One such film is from 2008, Henry Poole is Here The story centers around Henry Poole, played by Luke Wilson, who has recently been diagnosed with a terminal illness. Poole purchases a house in his old working-class neighborhood where he had a difficult and painful childhood. All he wants to do is to be left alone to live out his remaining days in quiet desperation. His plans also call for the consumption of mass quantities of vodka. Poole feels that life has dealt him an unfavorable hand, and there is little to do but to accept the reality of his situation.

Contrary to Poole's plans, his peaceful solitude is soon interrupted by his next door neighbor, Esperanza Martinez (Adriana Barraza), who believes that she sees the face of Christ embedded on the exterior wall of Poole's home. She is convinced that it is a miracle because drops of blood are exuding from the wall.

Soon Esperanza is organizing pilgrimages to see the miracle in Poole's back yard. Obviously, this does not set well for Henry's peaceful existence. Henry is an unbeliever as well as an atheist and rejects the notion of any type of miracle. He only wises to die in peace. Complicating matters is Poole's other next door neighbor, who has a small child that seems to be attracted to Poole. As the plot unfolds, there is a question of what is actually happening to the people who touch the image. Some believe they are being healed. Do miracles really happen? Can Henry Poole be touched even if he doesn't believe in the power of faith? And how do we choose to believe in things that we do not understand?

These are some of the questions that Henry Poole is Here poses. Any time you combine the subject of faith and miracles, you're sure to open yourself up to criticism. And with that said, most film critics had a field day condemning this film as nothing more than a complete waste of time.

Was it the subject material or the technical or artistic merits of the film that bothered the critics? I would agree that Henry Poole is Here may not be Oscar-worthy material, but it is a solid effort that, for the most part, hits the mark. This is one of Luke Wilson's better efforts to date. And the supporting cast is clearly on target.

Henry Poole is Here is a very spiritual movie and has the ability to touch not only believers but agnostics and atheists as well. This film is authentic and real and a story everyone can respect. Few mainstream Hollywood films offer a positive view on faith. *Henry Poole is Here* avoids the usual pitfalls by not painting believers in a stereotypical manner— narrow-minded, right wing, religious zealots. The main Christian character, Esperanza, is seen as loving and exerts kindness and caring toward Henry. She has only his interests at heart.

Two of the key scenes in the movie illustrate the power of God at work in film. The first scene evolves around Poole confronting Esperanza on why she wants Poole to believe that a miracle is taking place and why it is necessary for her faith. Poole expresses his unbelief, resentment and doubt concerning the existence of God. The second scene is when

Patience played by Rachel Seiferth expresses her desire to choose to believe in her miracle. This scene is a quiet example of how to share our faith in the small, meaningful moments, which most of us don't recognize.

If you are looking for a film that is strange, thoughtful and unusual, then Henry Poole is Here is a good choice. Perhaps the real miracle of this film is believing in something bigger than ourselves and the willingness to accept it. Maybe just discovering the joy of life once again, in and of itself, is a real miracle. For film goers, Henry Poole is Here is truly a miracle because we do not see films that are willing to explore matters of faith, belief, doubt and the healing power of God from mainstream Hollywood. That is truly a miracle.

Chronicles of Narnia: The Voyage of the Dawn Treader

Like most people, I read movie reviews, especially about movies I want to see. This can be good or bad. Often, reviews give away too much of the plot. And if the reviews are negative, are you still ready to plop down $10 of your hard-earned money? After reading several reviews of the latest Narnia installment, The Voyage of The Dawn Treader, I had mixed feelings. Most film critics said that it was mediocre at best, lacking character development as well as offering nothing more than a weak, tired story. They did give a positive nod to better overall visual elements and cinematography.

This raises an interesting question. Are the critics being fair or is there some form of bias at work? It's no secret that the Narnia series is based on Christian concepts. Walden Media directed a significant part of their promotional campaign toward a Christian audience. Are the critics reacting to their own bias toward Christian-themed films? In the case of The Voyage of the Dawn Treader, I would say yes. Also a case can be made for the fact that anyone who has not received Christ as his/her personal Savior would have a difficult time understanding or evaluating Christian or spiritual concepts. Therefore, nonChristian critics would undoubtedly have a difficult time of evaluating the merits of any of the Narnia films.

The bottom line is The Voyage of The Dawn Treader is a solid film that offers good entertainment value with a strong but not overpowering message. It is a major step up from *Prince Caspian* but not on the same level as *The Lion, the Witch and the Wardrobe*.

The story goes something like this: Lucy, played by Georgie Henley, and Edward, played by Skandar Keynes, travel back to Narnia once again to assist King Caspian, who is searching for the seven lost Lords of Narnia. Along the journey is newcomer, Eustace, who is their younger cousin. The older siblings, Peter and Susan are now grown up and can no longer venture to Narnia because only children can enter this magical kingdom.

The Voyage of The Dawn Treader is the ship on which they embark upon the journey to the ends of the world in search of the Dark Isle where the seven Lords may be found. To make matters worse, an evil spell seems to be emulating from the island and spreading throughout the world.

The Voyage of The Dawn Treader is unique in one sense in that it does not offer a physical antagonist. There really isn't a bad guy or creature to contend with. This movie is really an allegory about man versus himself or the inner conflicts that we all deal with. It's ultimately a showdown between being tempted by our inner desires and fears versus following the will of Aslan, who serves as an analogy representing the will of God.

As any film student will tell you, movies dealing with inner conflict are not the easiest to tackle. Most people want a visible bad guy to direct their anger toward. However, the producers of The Voyage of The Dawn Treader have done a remarkable job finding the right balance between meaningful content and action while, at the same time, dealing with conflict at a personal level.

This isn't your typical fantasy film. Perhaps that's why Disney Pictures is no longer on board. Walden Media has made a conscious decision to remain faithful to the original writings of C. S. Lewis. Disney was hoping for the next Harry Potter series based more in action and adventure and less in substance. Most media reports pointed to differences over the overall budget as the reasoning for the breakup. But I'm convinced it was based on the original vision of the remaining five books.

Thankfully, in the last hour, 20th Century Fox stepped in to save the Narnia series. I think they have made a sound investment and have put the series back on solid ground. My advice is to forget what the critics are telling you about this film. It is well worth your investment of time and money. The Chronicles of Narnia, The Voyage of The Dawn Treader, is a delight. It is visually interesting, a joy to be part of an island-hopping quest for truth and freedom, and is a solid adventure for the entire family.

The Voyage of The Dawn Treader is the first of the series to be offered in 3-D. It certainly is not at the level the 2009 Avatar 3-D, but you will still enjoy this 3-D experience.

The Social Network

It was bound to happen sooner or later. With one out of every twelve people now a member of Facebook, someone was bound to do a movie about its origin. I have to admit that I was late to the game and just recently jumped on the bandwagon. But now with over 500 friends (and honestly I didn't realize I had 500 friends) I have become a fan.

By now, you realize the new movie, The Social Network, has become a phenomena of sorts. Some observers are going so far as to say that it defines an entire generation, much like *The Big Chill* did in the 1980s for baby boomers. It certainly is a leading candidate to take home a ton of awards at the upcoming Oscars. But is it as good as advertised? Should you go out and rent or buy a copy? At least, in my opinion, it has to be one of the best films of 2010. It's intelligent, smart and thought-provoking.

It's much more than just your standard corporate double-dealing and manipulation. Friendship, loyalty, jealousy and betrayal are depicted in just about every facet of The Social Network. The film is constructed in a fashion that constantly keeps you guessing as it cuts between present day and past events.

Who doesn't know a little something about the Mark Zuckerburg story? As founder of Facebook, he is the world's youngest billionaire. In The Social Network he is portrayed by Jesse Eisenberg, a brilliant computer wiz who is working on his undergraduate studies at Harvard University. We never fully understand why he starts Facebook other than an opportunity to meet girls. For that matter, we never fully understand his motives or why he is driven to do the things he does. That's what makes this film so brilliant. The viewer will have to determine that based on all the available evidence.

Zuckerburg is approached by fellow Harvard students, Cameron and Tyler Winklevoss, thanks to the magic of computer wizardry are played by Armie Hammer. He is asked to build a social network for college students. At the same time, his best friend Edwardo Saverin, portrayed by Andrew Garfield, helps to finance the new site and provide his business expertise. To make matters worse Napster founder, Sean Parker, played by Justin Timberlake, complicates matters by dividing the loyalties between Zuckerburg and Saverin. Obviously, the end result is a series of law suits and disputes over who is the real founder and owner of Facebook.

This kind of stuff can be really complicated. But the script somehow makes the details less important than the emotions that surround them. Is there a message to be found in The Social Network, perhaps a lesson to be learned? Often filmmakers themselves don't realize what kind of movie they are making.

The Social Network serves as a cautionary tale for all of us. It is a lesson we will learn at some point in our lives. Hopefully, we can learn from The Social Network and not in real life. Money has a way of changing everything. Put a few bucks on the table and see how people go absolutely crazy. Whether it's in relationships, ministry, or business, as soon as real money becomes part of the landscape, everything fundamentally changes. Often our humanity goes right out the window. The Social Network is a perfect example of how friendship and loyalty no longer matter. Now it's about backstabbing and getting the upper hand.

The real question is how do you justify your actions and find a way to live yourself once you have committed such acts. We know there is a price to be paid . Late at night it has to eat at the very soul of Mark Zuckerburg. Gee, wasn't there enough money to go around for everybody?

True Grit

Before I move forward with my views, opinions, or review of the new hit Western, True Grit, I have to make a confession. Westerns are one of my favorite genres. Honestly, I love almost every Western I have ever seen. So my thoughts on True Grit may be biased.

From the 1930s through the 1960s, Westerns ruled Hollywood. You could find a Western playing at your local theater any given week. Westerns fell out of fashion by the 1970s as contemporary audiences fell in love with special effects and action adventure movies. We saw a brief renaissance in the early 1990s starting with Kevin Costner's, *Dances with Wolves* followed by Clint Eastwood's, *Unforgiven*. Amazingly, both movies won an Oscar for Best Picture.

For those who love the Western genre, the 1990s brought a quick succession of one Western after another, including *Geronimo*, *Tombstone*, *Wyatt Earp*, *Wild, Wild West*, *Maverick*, and *The Quick and the Dead*. But in recent years, Hollywood once again turned its back on big-budget Westerns.

Thanks to the Coen Brothers, we are fortunate to see the Western once again grace the big screen. So let me get right to it. In my opinion, True Grit is the Best Picture of the year, period. And I would make that statement even if Westerns were not my favorite genre. The question that most people ask is how is this movie compared to the original John Wayne film from 1969, and is it better? Although it is the same movie and follows basically the same plot points, it is totally different in its style and tone.

The Coen Brothers decided not to base their film on the original 1969 film. Their version of True Grit reflects the original vision of the 1968 novel published by Charles Portis. This vision plays out beautifully in the opening graphic of the film which reads, "The wicked run away when there is no one chasing them", from Proverbs 28:1. Right from the beginning, we know that True Grit will be a film that's more about a spiritual journey than just a film about revenge and retaliation. The film eventually enters into a discussion about justice as it relates to revenge. The story is told from the viewpoint of Mattie Ross vs. Rooster Cogburn's viewpoint in the 1969 version of the film, which is a major difference from the original film. What also is different from the original film is that it is a much more personal story.

The new True Grit starts with the murder of Mattie Ross's father in Arkansas. Hailee Steinfeld plays the 14 year old, high spirited, headstrong daughter who is determined to seek justice for her father's death at the hand of the notorious Tom Chaney, played by Josh Brolin. Chaney has fled into the Indian territory. Ross is in hot pursuit looking for someone with "true grit" who can help her bring Chaney back to Arkansas to stand trial. She finds an unwilling ally in the likes of U.S. Marshall, Rooster Cogburn, portrayed by Jeff Bridges. Cogburn has a reputation for getting his man at any means, which usually means dead. Joining in the quest is Texas Ranger, LaBoeuf, played by Matt Damon. Along the way they will deal with an assortment of characters and outlaws. Mattie drives a hard bargain as she deals with the competing interests of Cogburn and LaBoeuf.

So what makes True Grit an outstanding movie? Is it the directing, acting, casting, cinematography, art direction, script or other factors? I don't care what film critics will tell you. There's no way to define outstanding filmmaking. In some ways, it's like the classic definition of pornography, "You know it when you see it". All of the elements come together in True Grit to create something that defines art. The individual elements somehow equal more than its total sum. And that doesn't happen very often in a movie.

True Grit doesn't work without an incredible career-defining performance by Hailee Steinfeld. She was only 13 years old when the film was shot. Not only does she deserve a nomination for an Oscar, but she gets my vote for Best Actress. The Coen Brothers auditioned over 15,000 girls for the lead. They realized they didn't have a picture without the right Mattie Ross.

The final narration from Mattie Ross brings a satisfying conclusion to the film's journey. "You pay for everything in this world. There is nothing free except the grace of God." Mattie's moral compass is determined to bring order to grace, mercy, justice, forgiveness and, ultimately, death itself.

Several people had raised eyebrows when it was announced that the Coen Brothers were going to produce a Western. Known for their eccentric and quirky approach to filmmaking, could they play it straight? Thankfully, they found a way to incorporate their creativity and their unique vision while at the same time paying homage to the Western genre.

It took the combined efforts of the Coen Brothers and the star power of Jeff Bridges, who recently won Best Actor for *Crazy Heart*, to remake one of the most popular westerns of all time a possibility. I can only hope that more directors will be willing to journey down this trail and embrace the Western genre. There are plenty of new stories to be told, and Westerns make a great backdrop and canvas to tell them in a uniquely American way. I believe Westerns are equivalent to Shakespeare's great theater. So do yourself a favor and make sure you see this film. It may be a long time before another Western comes along.

Inception

Inception is the rarest of all Hollywood movies—a truly original idea or concept. In an increasing age of remakes, retreads and sequels, Inception is indeed a breath of fresh air. It was released this past summer and was a shock to most industry insiders. Inception does not fit the profile of the typical summer blockbuster, which often offers nonstop action, explosions, and special effects. Don't get me wrong. This film does contain it's share of these elements; however, what separates Inception from most typical Hollywood formula movies is that it is smart, intelligent and though-provoking. Yes, it will require you to pay attention and to think, a lot.

Unlike most popcorn movies, Inception is about something. That something will be up to each viewer to discover and decipher. Frankly, it's quite surprising that a film of this nature would ever be released during the summer months. Warner Brothers Pictures took a huge gamble with a budget approaching $160 million in play. Having Leonardo

DiCaprio and director Christopher Nolan on board probably helped to ease the anxiety of the executives over at Warner. The end result was a smash hit. To date, Inception has grossed over $290 million domestically in North America. Let's hope other studios will take Warner Brothers lead in offering more original content.

Without giving too much of the story away, Inception takes place in a world where technology makes it possible to access the subconscious and invade an individual's dreams. Dominick Cobb, played by Leonardo DiCaprio, has been hired by Mr. Saito, a Japanese businessman played by Ken Watanabe. Cobb engages in corporate espionage for a fee. Cobb and his team are contracted to implant a thought into the subconscious mind of Saito's competitor, Robert Fischer, without his knowledge. The catch is Fischer must believe the thought originated in his own mind.

The only way this can be accomplished is by accessing a dream within a dream that is within a dream. It involves going down several levels of the subconscious to access the hidden parts of the mind. Along the way, Cobb and his team will face an array of obstacles because within our dreams are also our fears and painful memories that get in the way and must be reconciled. As I said, this is complicated stuff.

Some critics have argued that Inception isn't really that original—that it's all been done before in other movies. I think they have missed the point completely. Inception contains truth that is applicable to our present reality. Whether the filmmakers intended to say this or not, it is a reflection of the modern society in which we live. First, it suggests that we are all controllable. Second, there are forces or individuals that for their own means and purposes wish to control us. Third, for the most part, we are unaware of this. And, finally, as the title, Inception, suggests, an idea or concept can be planted into the subconscious and influence us. And on another level, the movie suggests that what we have buried deep in our subconscious ultimately will control our actions without our awareness. On a spiritual level, I'm convinced that a case can be made that today's media is engaging in the same activity portrayed in the film.

Inception proves that there is an audience for intelligent films. Inception will challenge you to question what you really think is true about what you believe and which reality is true. The bottom line is that if you are looking for a highly entertaining and visually-striking film that will keep you guessing, you will do no better than this film. It is currently available both on Blu-Ray and DVD.

Best Redemptive Films of the Decade

There are all types of "best of" lists, including comedies, westerns, action films, science fiction, drama, and musicals. But I want to offer up is a list of the most redemptive films from the past few tears. These are some of my personal favorites, films that you don't mind seeing over and over. I always find something new or interesting after each viewing. I believe the standard for a great film is watching it several times without becoming bored.

I chose redemptive films for my list because they are often the most powerful and inspiring movies produced. Done right, they can move us to be a better human being and lead us away from our self-destructive behavior. They can often challenge us to explore our life's pathway and the decisions we are making. In a Christian sense, redemptive films often lead us to salvation. In a broader sense, they are about becoming fully human and becoming fully capable of expressing emotions.

Redemptive stories are about change and huge character arcs. This often challenges screen writers to reach deep and take chances.

So let's get started. The first is **Walk the Line**, staring Joaquin Phoenix and Reese Witherspoon as Johnny Cash and June Carter Cash. Both of these actors get completely lost in their roles. It's a story where Johnny Cash could have easily fallen off the edge with a life of drugs and alcohol. But, as you may be aware, Cash became a devoted Christian and one of the most influential artists in the history of music. If you are a fan of Johnny Cash, you need to check this film out.

Reservation Road explores the aftermath of a tragic car accident. It looks at a universal theme we can all relate to, trying to get away with something that we know is wrong. It deals with guilt, forgiveness and learning how to move on.

To End All Wars features 24's Keifer Sutherland. It is perhaps one of the best examples of a redemptive story produced in recent years. It was released in 2001 and was considered a low-budget film that received inadequate promotion and marketing. That's too bad. It deserved a much larger audience. It's well worth your time to discover it on DVD.

Michael Clayton, for some, will be a controversial choice. It offers up a fair amount of bad language. But if you are looking for redemption, this film is a prime example. It stars George Clooney, who is one of my favorite actors. We may not always agree with his politics, but he certainly delivers the goods.

Clooney plays an attorney with a gambling problem. He is what's called a "fixer" for a major and prestigious law firm. His job is to make problems go away by any means necessary. The film was produced by the late Sidney Pollack, who was one of the best producers working in Hollywood.

If you are a Christian filmmaker and trying to understand the best way to be a media missionary, you need to check out **Bella**. This film is the type of movie that Christians should be making. It is a Christian film without being a "Christian" film. Bella was honored with the People's Choice Award at the Toronto Film Festival. It takes a hard look at self-forgiveness, reconciliation and redemption. I saw it first at the Biola Media Conference before its theatrical release. It was emotionally moving. It had a huge impact on me.

Never once did I think that the film had an agenda or was a message picture. Many critics criticized the film for that very thing. I totally disagree. Perhaps, the marketing and advertising plan could have been aimed at a broader audience. They should have let the film stand on its own two feet without tying it to the Pro-life movement.

Putting **Gran Torino** on my list will make a lot of Christians uneasy. I know it has some bad language, but that is not enough to disqualify it. The film was directed by Clint Eastwood, who also plays the lead role. Clint Eastwood's movies are always about something important. He is perhaps the best filmmaker over the past 25 years.

Here he plays Walt Kowalsk, who is a bitter, lonely, Korean war veteran and very much a bigot. This film explores the possibilities that we all have the capacity to change and to make great sacrifice.

Bruce Almighty features Jim Carey in the role of Bruce Nolan, who believes he can do a better job of being God than God. This movie is absolutely amazing. Here's a Hollywood, mainstream movie talking about free will, prayer and asking God to take control of your life. It's really hard to believe. It's done in such an entertaining fashion and at the same time takes a look at complex philosophical and theological issues. And frankly, can you go wrong with Morgan Freeman playing God?

Finally, **Family Man**. I love this film. It's a cross between *It's a Wonderful Life* and *A Christmas Carol*. "What if" films are always interesting. If you are looking for a great character arc, Family Man is your film. Family Man stars the always versatile Nicholas Cage as Jack Campbell, a man who does not understand the true value of life. This movie is an interesting look at what life could be like in a alternative universe.

Ok. That's my list. I'm sure I missed plenty of deserving films. What's your thoughts? Do you have any other redemptive films to add.

A MATTER OF PRAYER

Our mission here at Media Missionary School and Flannelgraph Ministries is to encourage you to pray for Christians and nonbelievers who work in the entertainment industry. We believe Hollywood and entertainment in general is a valid mission field. It is perhaps the world's most influential mission field. America's number one export is entertainment. So the question is what do we pray for.

Pray for all Christians who work in film, TV, media, internet—whether they be in Hollywood or the broader entertainment industry, church media, parachurch organizations, independent Christian filmmakers, educators, industrial video or local television stations. Pray that God's will be done in their lives and that they seek and understand their purpose and role in the industry. If God has called them to be elsewhere, pray that he will reveal that to them. But no matter the outcome, pray that they embrace a missional lifestyle, reaching those that God places in their path. Pray that they reach their friends, neighbors, relatives, business associates, vendors, or work associates. Pray that God gives them wisdom, discernment, knowledge, provision, favor, open doors, blessings, anointing, and that God place a hedge of protection around them and their families.

For those who are to be in the industry, pray that God will use them to reach producers, writers, directors, to production assistants and every one in-between. Pray that God will use everyone in the industry to create media that reflects God's truth and glory. Pray that God will use movies, television programs and other forms of media to reach audiences worldwide.

Pray for a new awakening and revival to sweep our nation and the world. Pray that God will raise up a new generation of media makers as media missionaries. Pray that he will equip, train and support media missionaries to Hollywood and the broader entertainment industry to create entertainment that reflects his truth and his message.

Pray that God will give this new generation wisdom, discernment , knowledge, favor, provision, and that God will place a hedge of protection around them as they enter into mainstream entertainment. Pray that they reach above and below the line in the industry, including, management, legal, distribution, marketing, promotion, and every other aspect of the industry.

Pray that God will use this new generation of media missionaries to transform and change the face of Hollywood and the entertainment industry. By doing so, they will transform our culture and the world itself. Pray that nonbelievers accept Jesus Christ as their personal Lord and Savior and dedicate their lives to pursue his truth. And, ultimately, pray for entertainment that causes people to reflect on their lives, the decisions they make and the pathway they have chosen to follow.

It's a big prayer and a big vision. It's what we have dedicated our lives to pursue here at Media Missionary School. Remember that nothing is accomplished except through prayer.

ENDNOTES

Chapter 1

No Endnotes

Chapter 2

[1] Wikipedia® is a registered trademark of the **Wikimedia Foundation, Inc.**, a non-profit organization.

Chapter 3

[2]Cincinnati Enquirer Newspaper, January 20, 2010

[3]Kaiser Family Foundation; Generation M2: Media in the Lives of 8-18 Year Olds; January 20, 2010

[4]Cincinnati Enquirer Newspaper, January 20, 2010

Chapter 4

No Endnotes

Chapter 5

[5]Wall Street, Oliver Stone Film, 20th Century Fox

[6]A Matrix of Meanings, Craig Detweiler and Barry Taylor; Grand Rapids, Michigan; Baker Academic, 2003

Chapter 6

No Endnotes

Chapter 7

No Endnotes

Chapter 8

No Endnotes

Chapter 9

[7]Neal Gobler, Life the Movie: How Entertainment Conquered Reality; New York Knoff, 1998

Chapter 10

No Endnotes

Chapter 11

No Endnotes

Chapter 12

No Endnotes

Chapter 13

[8]George Barna Research Group, *A New Generation Expresses Its Skepticism and Frustration with Christianity*, 2009

[9]Thom S. Rainer, The Bridger Generation, America's Second Largest Generation, What They Believe, How to Reach Them; Nashville, TN., Broadman and Holman Publishing, 1997

[10]The Dove Foundation Wesite

[11]The Barna Group, *Faith Has a Limited Effect on Most People's Behavior*, May 24, 2004

[12]George Miller, Michael Frost, Eyes Wide Open; Seeing God in the Ordinary; Sutherland, NSW Australia; Albatross Books, 1998

[13]Dr. Paul L. Cox, Heaven Trek; Copyright 2007 by Aslan's Place Publishers. All rights reserved.

Chapter 14

No Endnotes

Chapter 15

No endnotes

Appendix 1

Appendix 2

Appendix 3

ABOUT THE AUTHOR

Harold Hay is an award-winning writer, producer, and director who lives in Florence, KY with his wife Karen of 33 years. He has produced numerous television shows including, 180 Videos and The Zone, which aired on over 200 stations in North America and 15 television networks worldwide. His programs have been honored by both the NRB and GMA for Best Program of the Year. He also has created a faith-based educational program for high school students who are interested in pursuing a career in media, film, or TV. Currently, he is the President of Flannelgraph Ministries and the founder of Media Missionary School, an online website and blog dedicated to the raising up, equipping, training and supporting future media missionaries to the mainstream entertainment industry.

www.ingramcontent.com/pod-product-compliance
Lightning Source LLC
Chambersburg PA
CBHW062136280526
45788CB00001B/190